VOLAR

"As an avid reader of leadership books, I can confidently share that people of all ages, experience and backgrounds will benefit from the personal insights and advice that Mitch shared throughout *VOLAR*. She expertly points out that determining and then leaning on your resources is key to growth and development, something we encourage in Sales and Service at The Tampa Bay Lightning. This is an essential read if you are looking to better yourself personally and professionally."

**–Travis Pelleymounter**,
VP Ticket Sales and Service, Vinik Sports Group

"*VOLAR* is the biggest, simplest idea that has ever hit the scene for effectively overcoming adversity and roadblocks in any aspect of your life. Mitch Savoie Hill's formula will help you 'soar' and achieve your goal no matter how big or small."

**–Danielle Duran**,
Director Member Services, Los Angeles Chargers

"Leading a diverse and inclusive team is an honor and by implementing Mitch's powerhouse approach to engagement, your team will achieve optimum success!"

**–Brett Henderson**,
Branch Manager, United Rentals

# VOLAR

Soar fearlessly!
Mitch

# VOLAR

## How to Turn Roadblocks Into Runways to Success

**Mitch Savoie Hill, CPC**

**BOOK**LOGIX®
Alpharetta, GA

This publication is meant as a source of valuable information for the reader, however it is not meant as a substitute for direct expert assistance. If such level of assistance is required, the services of a competent professional should be sought. The author has tried to recreate events, locations, and conversations from his/her memories of them.

ISBN: 978-1-6653-0335-4 - Paperback
eISBN: 978-1-6653-0336-1 - eBook

Library of Congress Control Number: 2022903497

Printed in the United States of America                    0 2 2 2 2 2

This paper meets the requirements of ANSI/NISO Z39.48-1992 (Permanence of Paper)

Headshot photo used with permission by Aswini Oliver, TEDx Alpharetta Women Organizer

*To my soulmate, best friend, and biggest cheerleader,
Jason Edward Hill, whose support helped this book come
into existence.*

# CONTENTS

## PART THREE - Lean On Your Resources

## PART FOUR - Actualize a Plan

## PART FIVE - Recalibrate When Necessary

# INTRODUCTION

This book is meant to be a powerful bag of magic tricks or a hefty box of craftsman tools. It can be used in several ways.

For someone facing adversity or struggling to make sense out of current or past roadblocks along the road to a dream, this book can be your guide.

For someone leading a team, this book can help you figure out how to engage and rally each team member around a vision and a plan of action toward that vision, despite roadblocks. This book is as much about personal leadership as it is about one who leads many. Leadership is leadership. If you can manage yourself—your thoughts, decisions, and personal goals—you can help others do the same.

This book can also be for someone who needs hope, a spark of light to illuminate the way out of a dark tunnel en route to a dream. Or it may be for someone trying to find their true purpose—that thing that gets us out of bed in the morning with a jump and a smile. Don't have that yet? Don't fret. This book can help.

The exercises in this book are gleaned from over twenty-five years of training staff members, mentoring managers, and coaching clients, many of them executives with diverse teams and challenging goals. Some of them were people at a crossroads, trying to make a major transition and not knowing exactly how.

The stories shared herein, some of which are very personal, are meant to be illustrative and provide examples of the concepts and tools that are VOLAR—tools that will help an individual or a team turn their adversity into their advantage, their roadblocks into runways to success.

What this book has done for me, personally, is give meaning to some of the rough and painful parts of my own journey to success and happiness. It was written out of gratitude for what I have survived, and for the multitude of blessings life always provides. It proved that my adversity is my advantage, as long as I can use it to learn and to help others.

I hope you will find value here, make impactful realizations, and then pay it forward. For I believe our worth can only be measured by how much positive impact we can impart on others and on the world at large.

As individuals working alone, we struggle to survive; together, we thrive!

## CHAPTER 1

# VOLAR

### Your Adversity Is Your Advantage

HOW COULD THAT BE? How could your adversity or your company's adversity be your advantage? Perhaps that sounds absurd. Are you facing a roadblock right now that seems permanent? Perhaps you have surpassed great adversity in your life already? I have no idea what you have suffered and survived but, if you are reading this now, somehow you have survived. You are a victor!

Adversity comes in many forms. It could be the loss of a job or the loss of a loved one. It could be a stop sign or an unexpected detour that throws you completely off track. Ever had that happen? Even if you have a compelling vision and a goal that drives you every day, whether you are currently on the path to achieving it or just feeling its fierce pull, adversity will test you. Roadblocks will appear. The great news is they don't have to stop you in your tracks. Great goals come with great tests, tests of your will and ingenuity. It helps to surround yourself with people who support your vision and to establish guidelines that will aid in your journey from vision conception to reality to celebrating your achievement!

## Adversity Doesn't Have to Thwart nor Define You

When I was a child, I lived in New Jersey with my very young single mother and my baby brother, Michael. My mother struggled to feed us despite the help she received from welfare—which was not as much as some people would think. She had separated from my father when I was barely one year old. A few years later, she had my brother with a man she hoped would be a good father to us both. Although he was a kind and jovial man, he struggled with a vicious disease—alcoholism—one he would not vanquish until decades later. This left my mother no choice but to send him on his way early on in my brother's life. My mother believed she was better off alone than in bad company—"*Mejor sola que mal acompañada.*"

So, she struggled alone, in a low-income, roach-infested apartment in Paterson, New Jersey. She had moved us from my birthplace, sunny Miami, to follow her mother and siblings. I hated that move.

The winters in New Jersey were brutally cold. I hated the cold. Snow was pretty but it did not feel good. We couldn't afford good heating or much food. My mother did the best she could with her circumstances. She was a survivor. With barely a high school diploma, she struggled to find work—odd jobs, temp factory positions, and even cleaning restaurants at night—while I took care of my baby brother.

I was seven; I was underweight, malnourished, and suffered constantly from bronchitis. My diet consisted of a *lot* of grilled cheese sandwiches (well, I'm not sure this giant block of fluorescent orange—in our neighborhood, they called it "gov'ment cheese"—was actually cheese). We also ate a lot of this cheap cereal—I will not drop any brand names here, but suffice to say it was aptly named for the explosive effect it had on our stomachs. The box had this scary-looking clown on it and the cereal was unnaturally bright and colorful. It always wreaked havoc on our digestion. Life in general was harsh.

Then, when I was nine, my paternal grandmother,

Lilia Rosa Gandul, took me in. I had been staying with her for the summer, as had become our annual routine, when she offered to make my seasonal stay into a permanent one. She understood my mother was struggling and felt compelled to help. This woman was my super-heroine, a woman who looked adversity in the eyeballs numerous times in her life and challenged, "Is that all you got?" She blasted through all roadblocks!

Lilia fled Cuba when Fidel Castro firmly installed himself as its dictator. She left everything she knew and loved behind to seek refuge and freedom in America. She arrived in Miami, via New York, with nothing but her babies in hand and no formal education. However, what she did have was a clear vision for herself and her family, and she possessed unwavering faith. With that faith, excellent critical thinking skills, and an incredible way of connecting with people, she went on to build and operate several successful businesses, own her dream house, and help a multitude of people along her life's journey. I learned a lot from my grandmother Lilia about turning roadblocks into runways to success. I also learned about work ethic, charity, solid morals, and a formula for success. She created *her* own story and achieved great things against hefty odds, a testament to what you can do if you decide that:

**YOU create YOUR story.**

My mother also went on to create her own story, changing her circumstance for the better. Eventually, she went back to school and became a licensed medical assistant. She has since lived a life of service through her love for her profession and the people she has helped throughout her long career.

*What do I know of adversity?*

Too much, unfortunately. Perhaps not as much as others. Perhaps much more than most. Who is to measure pain and suffering? (Well, besides the personal injury lawyers, I guess.) The fact is we all face some kind of roadblock at some point. I was well acquainted with adversity early on in my life. At some point, I had to decide what I would choose to be—victim or victor. I understood that victimhood is really not very fun, and I kinda like fun. So, I learned to adapt, to seek meaning in the pain, an advantage in the adversity. My best friend, Yaddyra Peralta, once told me: "You are a master at making premium lemonade out of lemons!"

I had a hearty laugh! Of course, being a poet, she has an incredible way with words. It's true though—I *have* learned how to take the lemons provided to me and turn them into premium lemonade. You can learn how to do the same. You can learn how to fly—VOLAR!

## VOLAR

<u>Volar</u> is the Spanish word that means "to fly; to soar."

Have you ever had a dream where you focus intensely on levitation and eventually make your whole body rise off the ground, especially if there is imminent danger? As a child, I would often have vivid dreams of flight that felt so real, I would sometimes wake up with a violent jolt—as if I had suddenly hit the ground. I wanted so desperately to be able to fly.

Perhaps my obsession with flight had something to do with my turbulent childhood. Throughout my life, I had to fly away from many things—childhood poverty, physical and emotional abuse, toxic relationships, horrible bosses, and other dangerous situations.

### What Dangers Have You Had to Fly Away From?

Perhaps you are in it right now, struggling to see the path out. Perhaps you've been stuck for so long that a path out isn't even imaginable. Are you stuck in a terrible relationship, stuck in a dead-end job, or stuck in a great job but finding that it just doesn't fulfill you? Situations like these can make you feel like you are dissolving, losing your identity or hope. It is hard not to feel sorry for yourself when you are the object of abuse. Some people around you even feed into it by offering sympathetic looks and comments— "Oh, you poor thing." This sympathy, by the way, is NOT constructive. This kind of sympathy seems to validate what you already feel like—a "poor thing," powerless, unable to control the situations around you. But the truth is that you *do* have control. You may not have control over a situation or the current state of things. You may not be able to control the sudden death of a loved one, a worldwide pandemic, or your company going out of business, leaving you suddenly unemployed. However, here are three things you *can* control:

1.  How you <u>react.</u>

2.  What you <u>tell</u> yourself about the situation.

3.  What you <u>decide</u> to do next.

Here is the first lesson I offer in terms of handling adversity:

> **When adversity rears its ugly head,**
> **don't ask *why*?**
> **Ask *what* instead.**

Do not ask *"Why"* — Why now? Why ME? Why, GOD, WHY?!

Instead, ask *"What"* — What now? What next? What can I learn from this? What open door will this closed door afford me?

Ask "WHAT?" instead of "WHY?" Make the decision that you will not be the spoil of adversity, but that you will fly beyond it: VOLAR!

**VOLAR** is not just a word. It's a formula, my own special recipe, each letter an ingredient in the process of overcoming roadblocks to your goals, creating runways, and taking flight toward the things you dream of. Today, as an executive coach and professional speaker, I have found the advantage in my adversities by sharing what I have learned. This gives meaning to all that I *have* survived.

In this book, I will share simple yet powerful and immediately actionable tools in hopes that it will help you, as it has done time and again for me and for the clients I serve, to turn your roadblocks into runways to your success!

## How to Use This Book

**VOLAR**: Here is a quick introduction to this formula for success before we dig deeper into the chapters to come.

**V**ision

**O**pportunity

**L**ean on your resources

**A**ctualize a plan

**R**ecalibrate when necessary

I will break VOLAR down for you, share some stories to illustrate how it works, and offer some exercises to help you apply it. I use these exercises regularly and successfully with my coaching clients and personally. I hope to inspire in you the desire and willingness to develop and test out your own wings. It is such a wondrous gift to be able to learn from your adversity and use it to the advantage of yourself and others. To do otherwise is to sink into victimhood and apathy.

> ### Mitch's Words of Wisdom:
> The difference between *failing* and *prevailing* lies in the way in which we handle life's sudden side-swipes—how we <u>react</u> to the situation, what we <u>tell</u> ourselves about it, and what we <u>decide</u> to do about it.

It is totally understandable if you do not know how to overcome whatever obstacles you are facing right now, whether personal or professional. This is why I decided to become a certified professional coach and also why I, myself, have a coach. We do not make it alone. I have had great teachers, mentors, and friends that have helped me along the way. I am here to help you now, to pay it forward. One day you will pay it forward, too. Combined talents, experiences, and efforts make for a greater whole— greater power! Together we are better. Together we learn, grow wings, and soar!

I know it could sometimes feel like your goals are impossible to reach, but if a goal is worth achieving, you can get there. It just takes *Vision*, being open to the right *Opportunities*, being willing to *Lean* on your resources, being focused enough to *Actualize* a plan, and being brave enough to *Recalibrate* when necessary.

This book is for those with a fighting spirit, the courage to dream, a child-like curiosity, and an indomitable will toward a life of success and joy.

Your journey can be what you envision it to be. Do you want to be a successful executive, business owner, rocket scientist, or parent? Whatever you want to achieve, it is totally up to you. I will provide the tools and the flight plan. You fill in the coordinates.

## CHAPTER 2

# Roadblocks

HAVE YOU EVER BEEN traveling down a path and suddenly been thrown off by an unexpected obstacle or tragedy—a *roadblock*? How did you deal with it? What did you tell yourself in the moment? How do you normally deal with adversity? Do you have an emergency plan, steps to help you find your bearings and keep moving forward? If you don't, you are not alone. Many people do not.

I often coach property managers and I ask them: "Do you have an emergency plan for your properties? If there is a sudden fire, water loss, or active shooter, do you have a readied plan of action written out for all to easily follow?"

They nod: "Of course! What kind of property manager doesn't?"

Then I ask: "Do you have an emergency plan for your own life, your own emergencies or sudden losses?"

*Crickets*

Life has been dealing out adversity since the beginning of time, and yet, why do we always seem so surprised when it happens to us? Isn't that usual in the game of life? Do we know exactly when we are going to face a serious illness, see a loved one die, or have a company go out of business because of a natural disaster or a pandemic that suddenly breaks out? Can we see into the future with such detail that we're never caught off guard? If so, I would like to ask you about some lottery numbers!

How could we foresee emergencies? We can't. Yet most people do not have a personal emergency plan ready to break out and execute, like many people do not have an emergency fund in the bank.

VOLAR is not only a step-by-step guide for making dreams a reality, it is also an integral part of any emergency plan. You just have to pull out the plan, think through the steps, then execute.

In November of 2011, I found myself suddenly homeless. HOMELESS! I mean, when I woke up that morning, I had a place to live and when I got home from work, I did not. An unfortunate event forced me to grab my things and get out of the place I was renting without notice. I had a boatload of debt, no money in savings, and nothing in the bank—I mean I had NOTHING. What would you do in that moment?

I did what I think any sane person in my place would have done—I panicked, sat in my car, and sobbed!

Then I heard my grandmother Lilia's voice in my head. She had passed away a few years prior, but she always seemed to be with me when I needed her most. That day, she was telling me: *"Mas se perdió en la guerra."* (More was lost in the war.)

That's what she always used to say if you were lamenting about something lost or some thwarted goal. Got a bad grade on a test? The boy you had a crush on is now ignoring you?

*"Mas se perdió en la guerra."*

The war she was referring to was the 1959 Cuban/Castro Revolution, which stripped people of lands and severely restricted the freedoms that were previously enjoyed in Cuba, leaving my family no choice but to escape to the United States. My people had to leave everything they had behind—all their possessions, their homes, everything they knew, and even some family members that weren't so lucky to get out. In my mother's case, at seven years old, she and her baby brother were sent off to unknown relatives in the United States while my maternal grandmother was held back in a Cuban jail for rebels. Her crime? Having her children secretly leave the country with their father, who was openly against Castro's rule. She wouldn't escape Cuba until years later.

My people had survived unthinkable adversity, forced to leave their beloved homeland behind. In contrast, I simply had to leave an apartment.

*"Mas se perdió en la guerra."*

Those words always seemed to put things into perspective in my life.

Still, there I was. Homeless in LA with no immediate solution.

In difficult times like this, where do you go? What do you turn to in order to sort your thoughts and consider your prospects? I believe you need to go to your *thinking place*. Everyone should have one. It's the place you go to when you need to get some space and think through some solutions or bright ideas. My thinking place has always been the beach.

As I sat on the sand, right by the Santa Monica Pier, listening to the roar of the Pacific, my next move unclear, I thought to myself, *Where do I go from here?*

How did I get there? That's quite a story. More

importantly, how did I fly beyond that temporary-yet-*major* roadblock and go on to become an executive in multiple industries, debt-free, with money in the bank, and eventually establish and run my own business? VOLAR.

### Mitch's Words of Wisdom:

**We achieve what we can conceive.**

You've probably heard this or some iteration of this before—the concept that you get what you focus on, good or bad. I believe this to be true. But sometimes we encounter . . . Roadblocks!

We stumble across adversity along the way to achieving our dreams.

I know a little more than something about adversity. I am the child of Cuban exiles. I have survived poverty, isolation, toxic relationships, horrible bosses, and even—in this case—homelessness. Yet somehow, while I was *in* it, I always envisioned myself beyond the roadblock and *used* that vision to propel me forward to success.

We all have our stories, and most of us eventually encounter some roadblocks.

> What is your biggest challenge right now? What do you wish you could change or improve? It may be loneliness, longing for meaningful relationships, or it could be that you are facing a steep goal at work and don't feel totally confident in your abilities to achieve it. Perhaps you are facing a crisis of identity: "Who am I?" "Is *this* what I am really meant to do for the rest of my life?"

Adversity is not always an external force. Sometimes it is your own limiting fears ruthlessly fighting against your strong desire to break out of the life someone else carved out for you, a life that just doesn't inspire you. You feel like you've checked off all the boxes someone else laid out, but you're left feeling empty and unimpressed. Yet somehow attempting to fly out of that limiting box is too terrifying.

In December of 2019, I took a leap of great faith and decided to walk away from my six-figure-income corporate career to focus on my vision: SavHill Consulting LLC—my own coaching and speaking business. Who could have guessed that just three months later, the WHOLE WORLD would shut down? The WHOLE world—quarantined?! I mean, who prepares for *that* in a business plan? Roadblocks!

*How do you deal with that?*

Well, people deal with adversity in different ways:

- Do you find someone to blame?
- Do you fall into crippling despair?
- Do you slip into overwhelm and just give up?

I'll tell you what I did. First and foremost, I made a decision!

### Mitch's Words of Wisdom:

**Decision precedes action.**

I decided that I was *not* going to give up, no matter what, not after having taken such a brave jump! I decided I was going to activate my emergency plan—VOLAR.

Next, I hired a business coach. Some people thought I was making a counter-intuitive choice to spend that money in the midst of a global pandemic. Well, I knew better. Being a coach, of course I believed in the benefits of coaching. More importantly, I had to believe in myself. I also knew what my vision was and that it was time to lean on some resources—a coach being one powerful resource. Sometimes you need a little help, whether it's hiring a coach, finding an accountability partner, or just talking things through with someone you trust. None of us make it alone. This is yet another reason why I wrote this book. This is why I coach and mentor.

> ### Mitch's Words of Wisdom:
>
> If you often make yourself a great resource to others, you will find no shortage of resources when you need one. That is the farmer's law— you reap what you sow.

I hired a coach to help me figure out my next steps, inspire some bright ideas, keep me motivated, and hold me accountable. It was the best investment I made for myself and for my vision. In a year in which many companies were going under, I was able to grow my speaking/coaching business and even land the dream opportunity of delivering my first TEDx Talk!

Counter-intuitive? On the contrary! I went with my gut, my intuition, the inner voice that sometimes whispers and other times *yells*. Intuition is your barometer.

Have you ever gone against your intuition and regretted it miserably? I have too many times— enough times to finally know better! When adversity sideswipes you, leaving you in a daze, it is intuition that sometimes pulls you through to the other side, intuition coupled with a strong vision. When those two powerful elements work hand in hand, magic occurs! Like having a TEDx Talk just fall into your lap.

At some point, we all face adversity, tragedy, roadblocks, whether they be personal, cultural, family-related, or as a business. Even our own thoughts, particularly impostor syndrome, can be a major roadblock to our success. Thus is the game of life. It wouldn't be a game if it didn't come with some challenges.

> Think about a time when you faced adversity. Now think about how you dealt with that adversity. Did you back down? Did you overcome and learn something from it? How was your adversity possibly a step into something unexpectedly advantageous? How could you use your adversity to help others who are now struggling with the same or a similar situation?

VOLAR is about overcoming challenges to your vision or your team's vision. It is also about *perspective* and *decision*. You have to decide to win, no matter what, to free yourself if you feel trapped, to fly past the roadblocks because your happiness and success depend on just that. You will never make anyone else happy if you cannot start with yourself.

Just as I did when I decided to keep my business running during a worldwide pandemic, you need to make a strong decision *not* to give up on your vision. Do not allow any roadblocks to stifle you. Remember:

## Decision Precedes Action.

So, have you made the strong, unshakable decision to be successful? To be happy? Are you willing to do everything in your power to turn roadblocks into runways to your success?

If so, here we go. Get excited! You are about to learn how to FLY!

# PART ONE

# Vision

## CHAPTER 3

# Vision

### The V Is for Vision; Clarify Your Vision

IT ALL STARTS HERE, with a clearly defined vision of what exactly you want to accomplish. You can't erect a building without precise blueprints, right? Maybe you already know this. Maybe you think, *Everyone knows this!*

Oh yeah? So why aren't there a billion billionaires?

Many people believe that the reason they do not achieve their dreams is because they struggle to stay motivated, like starting a diet with fervor and then giving up three weeks later. I will offer that the *real* reason people do not achieve their dreams is because they do not clarify the vision to begin with. It is like getting into a car, cranking the engine, pulling out of your parking spot, and pressing the accelerator to move forward with no idea where you are actually trying to go. Before the *how*, you have to have the *where*. *Where* are you going? What is your final destination?

You want to lose weight. OK. Exactly *how much* weight? What is your healthy weight, anyway? How many pounds should you lose per week? And when you do lose that weight, what then? How will you feel? Then envision a step further—how will you sustain it? Is just "losing weight" the real vision, or is there more to it than that?

Clarifying a vision is like disassembling a Russian doll, right down to its final, little piece. As a coach, this is one of the first steps I work on with my clients—distilling down the specifics of their vision so it is simply stated. Break your vision down and make it feel *real*. So real that you have a clear mental picture with sights, sounds, and emotion—that's right, emotion. What is the emotion you want to *feel*? Accomplishment? Exhilaration? Love? You have to get the feeling of enjoying that final destination. What would life look like, feel like, *be* like? What security, comfort, or joy would your vision bring about? What would you contribute as a result? Naming a goal is not enough. You have to get very clear on it, then *write* it into existence, *speak* it into existence, and *post* it on a wall so it stares you in the face every day.

After more than one failed marriage, kissing a ton of frogs, and feeling total despair at the thought that I would never find the perfect partner to share my life with, I decided to do a little vision exercise. I realized that the reason I kept falling into bad relationships is because I was settling for less than my ideal partner. But what *was* my ideal partner? How could I find him? And if I did find him, how would I know for sure? What if I wasn't clear on exactly what it was I even wanted in a partner?

Here is what I did:

First, I wrote out all the exact qualities and values that were important to me—how this person would make me feel, their sense of humor, their musical preference (he had to love Dave Matthews). I clearly defined everything I could think of in a perfect match for me.

Then, every night before I went to sleep, I would spend some time visualizing him—how he would look at me, lovingly touch my face, smile at me with admiration in his kind eyes. I pictured us dressed up for some affair like the theater or listening to Dave Matthews together (I said *specific*!). I would feel honored, respected, and loved unconditionally, while feeling the same for him. That written and mental exercise is what prepared me to meet *this* man. It is what informed me, beyond a shadow of a doubt, that it was **him** the moment we first engaged in conversation—after he tapped me on the shoulder at a Dave Matthews Band concert!

Years later, I found that list I had made and read it to him, just for fun. His eyes grew wide with surprise.

"You just described *me*!"

I smiled. "I know! But look at the date on this journal entry!" I had written it months before we met. Vision accomplished!

## The 3-Ds

Your vision should be in 3-D, meaning you have to be able to visualize it in real time, see it coming to fruition, and feel yourself actually crossing the finish line.

Your vision also has to have *the 3-D's*:

- Detail
- Drive
- Decision

## The First D: Detail

Break your vision down to its nuts and bolts. The vision has to be so clear that it is burned into your brain as reality.

Clarity is vital. You have to distill and clarify—be specific.

It is impossible to formulate a plan if you don't have a clear idea of what exactly you are trying to achieve. It is like taking out a pot to cook in, spreading out random ingredients, and tossing them in willy-nilly with no idea of what you are attempting to prepare. If you get extremely lucky, you may come up with a masterpiece, but chances are more likely that you will have an inedible hodge-podge that will even have your needy rescue dog turning up their nose.

I have had coaching clients say something like, "My goal is to increase sales!"

To which I respond with a question, "What's the number?

"What do you mean?"

"What's the exact number you are trying to hit? How much of an increase? What is realistic over last year's?"

"Well, I am not sure."

"OK. What was last year's number?"

"Uh . . . well, I just started this job . . . I'm not actually sure."

How can you set sales goals without knowing what the exact target is? This is where I have them go back and do their homework! Do some deep research before we talk further about their vision.

You have to have a detailed goal if you are going to make a plan to get there.

A colleague of mine is a top producer for one of the largest paint companies in the world. He posts his weekly goals on a small piece of paper in his car visor. This way, his goals are staring him in the face all day as he is driving around making client calls. The result? He always makes his goals.

## The Second D: Drive

The Drive is your "why."

Why do you want this vision to materialize?

Why are you motivated about the goal or vision? What would happen if this goal came to fruition? What would happen if it did not?

**\*Note:** I will give you a little homework. I invite you to take some time later and write out everything that comes to mind in answer to the questions above. Success and failure can both be great motivators. The thought of succeeding, of feeling accomplished, and receiving all the things that come with that big goal can pull you through the toughest roadblocks. On the other hand, the thought of **not** succeeding—of living a life without love or without purpose or without that feeling of accomplishment—can also be a major butt-kicker! Weigh out the two. Use these thoughts when you need motivation. Having your "why" will guide you, help tell you when you are off track, and help you vanquish the toughest adversities.

## The Third D: Decision

Decision is the mental agreement with yourself that you will **not** give up on working toward that goal or vision, despite adversity. Have no doubt—there will be adversity.

In 2009, while living in New Jersey with my brother, Michael, I felt this nagging and inexplicable gravitational pull to Los Angeles. I didn't really know anyone there except my high school friend Silvio, but I didn't expect to see him often. He had become a busy Hollywood executive producer for the hit TV Show *Ugly Betty*. I also had never really been to Los Angeles for any significant amount of time. Yet I had always felt a strong desire to go there.

I decided to give myself a birthday gift: a one-week reconnaissance trip to Cali. I had to figure out if the pull was real or if I would discover that I actually hated Los Angeles. The vision had started to formulate. I had my mind set on living on the coast in the Santa Monica/Venice area. I was so tired of the dark Jersey winters, the snow, the shoveling—ugh! I envisioned myself running on the beach every day.

That vision was the main source of my drive, initially. I would be running on the treadmill, after having shoved all my thick winter layers into a gym locker, and I would envision myself running on the sand, with the cool Pacific breeze in my face.

In November 2009, I booked the most affordable hotel I could find in Marina Del Rey, just a short walk to the beach where I could see the Santa Monica Pier overlooking the Pacific Ocean. When I arrived, excited like a kid at a theme park for the first time, I quickly changed into running gear and headed for the beach!

For the first time ever, it opened up to me as if from behind a theater curtain—the Santa Monica mountains towering over the vibrant, rambunctious Pacific, so alive, so full of creative energy, and so loud. I grew up between Miami and New York/New Jersey. I had been around the beach all my life, yet the Atlantic Ocean was so quiet and mild in comparison to this! It was energizing!

I recognized instantly where the pull had come from. I felt as though I had arrived at a familiar place that had been waiting for its prodigal daughter to return after a very long sojourn. It was surreal and exhilarating. It felt like *home*. In that moment, my vision was solidified. I made an irreversible decision, I was moving! I had my 3-Ds!

Now I just had to figure out how the heck my move was going to be possible. Lord knows I had some roadblocks to blast through! At the time, I was working as the lead trainer for an upscale national restaurant group by day, and spending every penny I made on making music, working hard to make it as a singer/songwriter by night. I had a backing band, played regular shows, and even took out a grossly high interest-rate loan to record a five-song album. I was giving my rock star dream everything I had, and I felt like it was going in the right direction. However, I also had a high debt-to-income ratio, and no money in savings—roadblocks!

So, how did I do it? Blast past those roadblocks to my west coast vision? More on that story later . . .

## CHAPTER 4

# Finding Clarity

## What If the Vision Is Not Totally Clear Yet?

HAVE YOU EVER HAD the feeling you were not where you were supposed to be, but had no idea *where* exactly you belonged? Maybe you want to make a transition but are not sure if the timing is right. Perhaps you just know you don't feel happy where you currently are. I encounter this often with my coaching clients. Some want to move up in their current companies but don't know how. Some want to start their own business but lack the confidence. Some want to switch roles but are too scared to make the change. Some just want to leap out and do something completely different altogether but are just not sure *what*.

That was me at the beginning of 2018. I had finally reached that life-long career goal of the "Six-Figure-Income Job." I was regional director of business development for a construction company. I was given total freedom to build and lead my own team, while also doing something that truly energizes me: being on stage! The stage, in this case, took the form of countless educational events wherein I was teaching HR-related classes to managers as part of my company's marketing strategy. These classes gave me the opportunity to develop business leads by connecting and engaging, while also allowing me to sharpen my presentation and leadership teaching skills.

What was there *not* to like? I made my own schedule, coached a great team of business development managers that were thriving, and got to be on stage teaching regularly while making a great income!

Why was it not enough?

Something in me was still not totally fulfilled. I wanted to do the parts of my job that I loved most—coaching, training, and speaking—and get paid well for it! I also wanted to be able to guarantee the product I was selling. If *I* was the product, I could control the quality. I wanted that total control and flexibility.

The first thing my inner, negative Mitch would yell at me was:

"Who the hell is going to pay you for that?"

The next thing my joyless, inner companion suggested was:

"There is no career like that!" (At the time, I was clueless about the professional speaker/coaching industry.)

So, I did an exercise I have my clients do now: wrote down all the activities that energized me, brought me joy, and aligned with my skills and experience. I wrote with a 3-D image in mind of myself doing what I loved—and I wrote a LOT. I was working on a vision, even if it wasn't clear yet. I had to have faith that I would know it when I saw it, like I did when I met my ideal partner at a Dave Matthews concert years prior. (It's a pretty powerful exercise!)

In August of 2018, after having worked out my vision in writing for months, I attended a conference in Orlando for the National Association of Women in Construction (Go NAWIC!) and was moved by the keynote speaker at the luncheon. I followed the speaker to her breakout session later that day. I could tell she was loving what she did: having fun with the audience while sharing valuable information and watching as they experienced some light-bulb moments! I was doing that a small percent of my time, but that day I thought, *That's it!* That's *what I want to do! Whether one-on-one or for a group, I want to inspire light-bulb moments and help create real changes in people's lives full time!*

Luckily, though the speaker was flying back out that afternoon, she was generous enough to offer me some time after class to ask specific questions. My question was simple: "How do I do what you are doing?"

She pulled up a chair, sat down, and patiently laid out my next steps if I was serious about doing this. I *was* serious! She suggested exactly what organizations to join, who to call, how to get certified as a coach, and what to expect when I entered this industry as a total newbie.

There it was, clear as a technicolor movie—the vision! *My vision!*

I knew it when I saw it because I had already written it down. At the time, however, I just didn't have all the pieces completely in place to bring the picture to life. That day the pieces fell into place. With my heart full of joy and excitement, and with a solidly outlined map, I began my new journey. Sometimes, it just takes seeking out the people that will help point out the way.

Just two years after that pivotal conversation, I had gotten certified as a professional coach, delivered my first TEDx Talk, and had my own thriving speaker/coach business, SavHill Consulting LLC!

As I tell my clients, don't worry if your vision is not 100 percent clear at first. Sometimes it starts with a gut feeling or a cloudy idea. The first step I will offer you is writing—*writing*, not typing (pen to paper activates a different part of your brain)—about what energizes you, what that new horizon would look and feel like, what your ideal day would be in this new place, job, relationship, etc. Writing will put the process in motion. The process involves getting exceptionally clear on what you want, and where you want to go. The more you put it in 3-D, the more the universe will send you more pieces to complete the puzzle.

As a coach, now I get to be a part of that process for my clients! I get to see the sparks fly when a well-placed coaching question prompts the ideas that lead to putting these puzzles together for them.

### The V in VOLAR is for "Vision— Clarify the Vision."

I get to help bring clarity to someone's vision and then help them turn that vision into reality. That process is always so exciting for me. It fulfills me to no end! *Now*, I am living my dream!

What fulfills *you* like that? What makes you excited to get out of bed in the morning and go? If it is not what you are doing right now, you deserve more! And it's possible, you may just need a little guidance.

Seek what you truly desire and it will meet you halfway to your horizon.

Clarifying your vision, as it relates to a goal, is not a lofty exercise or a dreamy wish list. It's about creating the final result in your mind, then on paper, and finally in the real, tactile world. Just like building a house, no builder builds without hours of planning and scheduling, without details all on paper first, and deadlines to live by. Also, no builder does all that planning work and then thinks, *Gee, I really hope this building will stand.* Of course, catastrophes can happen and unforeseen tragedies can throw a construction plan off the rails, but no one goes in expecting these scenarios. They go in expecting that what they draw out will become a real, solid building. Sure, you try to be prepared for roadblocks and sometimes a plan takes a swerve (we will talk about that later when we get to the R in VOLAR) but an architect does not hand in a design while assuming, "This is kind of lofty, I don't know . . . let's hope it works."

Think of yourself as the architect of your own life.

You *are* designing your future. You can create whatever you want within reason and within your scope of ability. Let's face it, I am never going to be a gymnastics gold medal winner in the Olympics—not in this lifetime. But that isn't nor was it ever my vision anyway.

> ### Mitch's Words of Wisdom:
> **Your true calling comes within the scope of your greatest gifts.**

What are your greatest gifts? How would these gifts be best put to use? What is the most impactful contribution you can make with what you've got?

Once you have those answers clearly in mind, you may just have figured out *your* vision. Once you have that, go into building that vision with the level of certainty a good builder possesses when building a house—with the idea that the house is already built. You just need to transfer it from paper to the three-dimensional world. All you need is the right tools.

EASY PEASY! YOU GOT THIS!

## CHAPTER 5

# Against All Odds

WHEN I WAS seventeen years old, a titan-strength vision led me to New York University's Tisch School of the Arts! The vision was so strong that I didn't even apply for any other school. I was not supported in my decision to leave Miami to attend NYU, mostly for very pragmatic reasons—my family couldn't afford it—but I knew nothing yet of smart financial decisions, nor did I fully understand the financial-aid package. You know, that "free money" I thought I had won? Woo-hoo! All I knew was that I had a vision—independent life and liberty in New York City!

The odds were heavily stacked against me. I did not have any technical training beyond high school musicals and drama class. I had taken a few guitar lessons before going rogue, opting out of boring theory to learn how to play rock songs like "Stairway to Heaven" by ear instead. And yet I was not about to let my lack of formal music and acting instruction hinder me from getting to my desired destination.

Around October of my senior year of high school, many of my fellow thespians were buzzing about an exciting opportunity. NYU's Tisch School of the Arts was coming to town and holding auditions for their program at one of the local colleges. Many were clamoring to sign up as there were limited spots available. But not me; I had a special advantage. I would spend summer and winter breaks with my mother in New Jersey, just twenty minutes outside of Manhattan, so this gave me the opportunity my high school colleagues in Florida did not have. Over the Christmas break, I auditioned for NYU *at* NYU! My mom and I traveled to Manhattan's West Village and arrived at a historic NYU brownstone overlooking Washington Square Park! It had creaky hardwood floors and ornate finishes on the walls that made us feel like we had traveled back in time to the 1800s.

In order to audition for the school's musical theater program, you had to present a song and a monologue. The song was a piece of cake—"I Dreamed a Dream" from the musical *Les Misérables*. I was obsessed with the book and show, had worked this song for a year in high school musical theater class, performed it at countless shows, and even won multiple prestigious awards in local and state evaluations. To say I was over-prepared and ready to kill with my song was *not* an understatement. *That* wasn't the problem. The problem was the monologue. I had **no** formal acting experience and didn't really know what constituted a good choice of content for an audition.

Audition day came. The song went as I had expected, despite my extreme nervousness. My mother said they could hear my voice ringing out in the hall where the parents and prospective students waited their turns. She exclaimed in her proudest Cuban/Jersey accent:

"That's my dawda in there!"

Despite being terrified, I felt really good about my song delivery. Unfortunately, I was not feeling as confident about what came next—the monologue. Nevertheless, I was going to do it full out! And so, it began.

The judges looked on with the straightest faces they could muster as I gave them my most enthusiastic rendition of the opening shower scene from the 1980s movie *Ferris Bueller's Day Off*! I kid you not!

In my preparation for this part of the audition, I had bought a book of famous monologues. It had everything from David Mamet and Arthur Miller to

Shakespeare, but it also had famous movie mono-logues—a real hodge-podge! Well, I wasn't too fa-miliar, nor too keen, on the serious plays and I had seen *Ferris Bueller*, so I chose the path of least re-sistance and memorized that thing a few nights prior to the actual audition.

It was a risk. A great, big risk. They must have thought, "Either this girl is totally crazy, or extremely brave."

Honestly, I may have been somewhere in between.

Tell you what though, my song must have really blown them away. In February of my senior year, I received my early acceptance letter from New York University! I was so excited, I screamed and jumped up and down in the kitchen, making my stepmother annoyingly snap, "*Ay! Que te pasa? ¡¡Estás loca?!*" (What is wrong with you? Are you crazy?!)

I shared my joyous news, giddy and out of breath from jumping too much. She wasn't impressed. Like I said, most of my family wasn't on board with this.

Still, I pored over the pages of my informational packet to wrap my head around my next steps. I was going to have to do this alone, figure it out for myself. I was okay with that. I would just *lean* on my resource—financial aid! Ah, young ignorance!

As I read through my acceptance letter, I was struck by something that didn't seem right. It informed me that I would be assigned to the Lee Strasberg Method Acting Studio.

Wait! What?

*Method acting*? I had applied for the *musical theater* program. I was confused. Had they not *seen* my monologue?

*They made a mistake,* I thought.

I immediately called to clarify, certain that they had just made a clerical error that could be easily corrected. I belonged in musical theater. The response was unexpected, "No mistake. Your singing is great. We felt you could use a little more focus on your acting." Heart slips to the floor.

Sometimes your vision is shifted just a little bit for you.

Despite that minor twist in the plan, and against all odds, I arrived in New York City in August 1992, and found myself attending my dream school—New York University! I was living in a dorm overlooking Washington Square Park, where I had auditioned just a few months prior. An immense sense of exhilaration and accomplishment washed over me. I had arrived. I was free. My vision had become a reality.

Never underestimate the power of a strong vision.

## CHAPTER 6

# Group Vision

**What If You're Trying to Motivate and Inspire a Whole Group around a Vision?**

FINDING OUT—with total clarity—what part of that vision is important to *each* individual, in a group, is how you get them on board.

It is not enough to simply name the vision.

"Okay, everyone, this is the quarterly goal we are going for! Rah-Rah-Rah!"

You have to make the vision *real* to them. They have to be able to see it, feel it, understand how this vision will positively impact *their* lives. What's in it for them? You may say, "Keeping their jobs—that's what's in it for them!" And you'd be right. But here is a question I often ask my executive clients—one they call *Mitch's Magic Coaching Question*:

"Do you want to be *right*, or do you want to be *effective*?"

The smart leaders always answer "*effective*"!

You can be "right" to the point of ruin. A team that is working with only the goal of "getting a paycheck" will do their very minimum requirement instead of creatively going above and beyond. They may comply begrudgingly or present you with problems, instead of being proactive. This type of team will never give you their very best. Sure, a paycheck is important; people will show up, clock in, follow your rules, and then clock out on the dot (or sneak out early), for a paycheck. However, if you want the very best out of a team, the most creative productivity, the willingness to work past the clock, the least number of problems, and little-to-no employee turnover, then you have to do more than lead with a title and a paycheck. You need to **lead with vision.**

Leading with vision means finding out what part of the company goal excites and motivates each member of your team, and then emphasizing that part! Especially when dealing with a diverse team, the more universal yet specific the vision, the better. You need to find out what motivates each member, and then tie that into the shared vision. You need to include every individual in that vision, listening to their input and *showing* (*show*, don't tell) that their input is valuable. This is how you get their buy-in— and you **need** their buy-in if you are going to accomplish anything great as a team.

One of my executive coaching clients wanted to present a strategic and challenging goal for her sales and production teams. However, when she communicated the goal, she received little response. She then decided to make it a game and offered a prize. Unfortunately, that got little response as well.

I asked her, "Have you surveyed the team for what they think is a good prize?"

She thought for a moment, "No, not really."

"Maybe you should start there," I suggested.

So, she did a little surveying of the team's interests. Much to her surprise, it turned out the team was disinterested in what she had originally offered up, even though *she* thought it was great. When she dug a little deeper, she also found that what struck a chord with one part of the team did not motivate the other. Each subgroup had different preferences— what one part of the team considered an exciting prize, the other had no interest in. When she elicited honest feedback, learned what was important to each group, and presented *that* as an alternative, she got traction. The game was on! The team began to work in a concerted and joyful effort toward their goal.

You can't assume what your team will find important. It is so easy just to *ask*, they'll *tell* you what is important to them. Is it paying for their kid's college fund? Putting a new roof on the house? Or a trip to Italy (that would be mine!)? I invite my executive clients to have a conversation, survey their team, and ask questions to truly get to know and understand what motivates each of them. Dig deep—truly get to know what is important to the individuals in your group, and then paint the vision with those colors. *That* is how you get excitement and creative cooperation.

The more diverse the team, the more inclusive the team culture and the more creative solutions to common roadblocks and success toward the group goal you will get!

Lead with the V—Vision. You will build great teams that rally around that vision and ultimately succeed!

## CHAPTER 7

# Different Strokes for Different Folks

WE GATHERED AROUND the beautifully polished, black baby grand piano that sat proudly in the raised section of my uncle's living room. My seven-year-old cousin, Iliana, sat at the piano bench, angry tears rolling down her face as she pounded the keys, punishing the poor instrument. Her father had interrupted her playtime with the cousins to beckon her to the piano before his guests and was demanding *"Toca La* Guantanamera*!"* (Play the *Guantanamera*!)

He was a proud Cuban businessman in 1980s Miami. The song was a traditional Cuban folk song, and it meant a lot to him as an exile. Having his daughter perform it on the grand piano in his living room for his friends was a display of his Cuban patriotism and of the status he had achieved despite being an exile.

I watched the scene with mixed feelings—pity for my cousin who looked so tortured, confusion as to why, and fiery envy.

My cousin and I were about the same age, but we had very different interests. I was very artistic with a penchant for music and dance. She was a rough-and-tumble tomboy who wasn't afraid of getting into fights and getting dirty. She wanted to play sports, like her brothers, but her father would not have it—"*Los deportes son para niños y marimachas!*" (Sports are for boys and tomboys!) This was some old-school Cuban ideology. It was not considered proper for young ladies to be outside getting dirty. Furthermore, only the most privileged young ladies got to take piano lessons. I knew it all too well. I was not so privileged, and it pained my music-loving heart terribly. So, they dragged her, literally kicking and screaming, to piano lessons. As I sat in the back seat of my aunt's car, confused but sympathetic to my cousin's pain, I wished above anything in the world that I could trade places with her! She would have happily accepted.

I had longed to play since I was two years old

when I was gifted a toy piano and learned to play "Mary Had a Little Lamb" right away. Iliana was the one who taught it to me. It was like magic, making music with this instrument! I would beg for lessons and always get the same annoyed response from my single and struggling mother—*"No hay dinero!"* (There is no money!)

It brought up a very important question about opportunity. Why did some have it and others not? Here was my cousin, with what seemed to be all the money in the world, as well as the opportunity I most desired, and yet it was her biggest nightmare.

It was my first harsh, real lesson about opportunity as it relates to money. I understood very little, but I did understand that my cousin had more—more toys, more fun snacks, more name-brand cereal varieties, more trips to the mall. She also had more *access*—access to opportunities like piano lessons because my uncle had money and we did not. *"No hay dinero!"*

I wondered, if I wanted the opportunity badly enough, would it ever materialize for me? Was there something I could *do* to create my own opportunities someday?

It was also a lesson in perspective.

Up until then, growing up in a low-income neighborhood where everyone was on welfare or as poor as we were, it didn't register that we had *no money*—except for my mother always angrily reminding me whenever I asked for anything, like a toy or a sweet treat. The kids in my neighborhood shared whatever toys they had. My best friend would wear one roller skate on her left foot and I would wear the other on my right, just so we could both skate, even if only on one foot. (This is a testament to how much we thrive when working with others. Who wants to skate alone?) We had fun with what we had, and despite not having fancy toys, we created our own fun. I made a "magic wand" out of a wooden stick and aluminum foil, wrote plays on scraps of paper, and we created all kinds of imaginary worlds out of the trees, flower patches, and bushes outside. Somehow having less made us more creative. We were happy children with what we had, despite my lack of an ever-coveted piano.

It was not until we visited my cousin that I encountered privilege and learned that there was a big divide, that some people had a lot more. However, I also learned that merely having *more* did not necessarily equate to happiness.

I figured out early on that success meant access to the things we want, but I also learned that not everyone wanted access to the same things.

While I envisioned happiness as a room full of musical instruments and the acquired knowledge to play them, this was hell to my cousin, whose vision of happiness perhaps was a dusty baseball field and the freedom to play just as rough and tough as her brothers did, or to be outside climbing trees instead of sitting at piano lessons.

Happiness begins with a vision based on what drives us. That drive pushes us to succeed, to lunge toward being the best. You cannot force your vision of happiness on someone else and expect them to lunge toward something if it does not drive them. You must find out what is *their* motivation. My cousin was forced to practice for hours every day and attend weekly piano lessons, much to her dismay. Yet she never *loved* it, not the way I would have. She could bang out the notes, and that is exactly what you heard that day when she was forced to "Play *La Guantanamera*!"—correctly placed angry banging.

How many of your team members, family members, your kids, or perhaps even *you* are going through the day just "banging out the notes"?

This is such a vital concept to grasp when trying to influence, invigorate, and inspire a group, a family, or even yourself:

Achieving a vision takes drive, and you must *truly* know what drives the *individuals* who are working together toward that vision.

Money is not the real answer. What the money represents exactly is what will spark effort. For some, that money represents freedom; like the freedom to break out of stereotypes and hold your position or freedom to play with the boys. For others, it is accessibility, like access to piano lessons.

What drives you? What drives your team? These are the first questions. This is where it all begins. This is the foundation of the vision. All goals and targets stem from there. This is where we start if we are going to find true success and turn roadblocks into runways. What is your "why"? What makes you want to fly?

## Vision Exercise

1. List out the activities that make you feel most energized, excited, exhilarated, and truly alive.

2. Now write why these things produce that sensation/emotion in you. What about these activities energizes you?

3. Keeping the above in mind, write out a clear, specific, and realistic vision/goal for yourself that would produce that response in your life.

4. Drill it down to even more specifics—what would you contribute, produce, exchange, and enjoy if you made that vision a reality? Write it down as if you are looking at it in real-time (in 3-D).

PART TWO

# Opportunity

# CHAPTER 8

# Opportunity

The O Is for Opportunity—When It Comes to
Your Door . . .

**When opportunity comes to your door,
you must raise your hand and say,
*"Si, por favor!"* (Yes, please!)**

BE VIGILANT FOR THE right opportunities. They
are all around us. But sometimes . . . we just don't
see them.

Sometimes we don't believe we deserve them, like
my first TEDx Talk. Remember I said it just "fell in
my lap"? Well, it didn't really just *fall* in my lap.

My grandmother Lilia used to say:

*"Uno no sabe para quien trabaja."* (One does not know for whom one works.)

She would say this, for example, when she had spent hours cooking a Cuban finger-licking gourmet meal just in time for a "lucky" family friend to show up, uninvited, in the nick of time, to be offered the "opportunity" to sit for this scrumptious dinner.

"Lucky?" I would whisper to her scornfully. "Seems like this guy gets 'lucky' every night!"

Abuela, or "Awe" as I called her, would laugh and say, *"Uno no sabe para quien trabaja."*

I wondered why she wasn't as annoyed as I was, these people just showed up and took advantage of the delicious situation! Awe, on the other hand, would find it amusing. It didn't bother her that this guy seized the opportunity to feast on her food because that is what she worked for. She thrived on seeing the joy people would experience from eating the food she had prepared with so much love. She never knew who would experience that joy from one day to the next, with people always showing up unannounced at dinner time. She just worked her art joyfully and left the rest up to God, as they say, not knowing entirely for whom she was working.

From the Bhagavad Gita, an ancient Indian holy book, I learned an invaluable lesson:

"Do what you love full out and leave the fruits up to God."

This means you should do what you love *without* concern about who will love it. The most awesome thing is the feeling of fulfillment and excitement you get from doing what you really love and what you are meant to be doing. If you do that consistently, the fruits of your labor just may fall in your lap when you least expect it.

In mid-2020, I focused fiercely on my daily activities of growing my speaker/coaching business—recording videos with helpful tips, posting verses in social media that I hoped would inspire my followers, and speaking for tons of organizations and groups. I was hoping that, though I did not know exactly for whom I was working, all that effort and outpour would attract great things to me.

It was that diligent and persistent outpour that led the TEDx Alpharetta Women event organizer to *me*, through social media. I couldn't believe it at first—well, actually, I couldn't believe it up until the day we did dress rehearsal! Have you ever shied away from an opportunity with all sorts of "valid" reasons—the "not ready enough," "not good enough," "not fill-in-the-blank-enough" feelings that deter us from jumping at great and scary endeavors? I will admit to you, my friends, that I felt all those things when it came to this TEDx Talk. I kept wondering when the organizer would finally realize that she made a mistake in offering me that speaker slot. I would present my draft, receive feedback, and think to myself, *Who am I kidding? I am out of my league here!*

Then I would rework the draft and present again, getting more feedback, trying to stay out of my head and leaning into the feedback, until I finally got the enthusiastic thumbs-up! And *still*, I didn't feel fully confident!

Have you ever felt like that? Have you ever felt like you were in the wrong room, wrong spot, wrong stage, or wrong role? My husband, Jason, would tell our friends, "The minute my wife got the news she was chosen to do a TEDx Talk, she got the worst case of impostor syndrome I have ever seen in her!"

He was right. I had envisioned this opportunity coming much later. I had thought to myself, *I still have a lot to learn*, and worse, *Who the hell cares about anything I have to say?*

In the end, I came up with something that at least *I* cared about. The subject ended up being a wonderful surprise, something unexpected and deeper than I had initially drafted. A talk about adversity and diversity, about the struggles of first-generation Americans, finding their identity, split between two worlds, multiple languages, and cultures. It was also about first impressions, snap judgments, and the limiting boxes we put ourselves and others in on a daily basis. Here is the kicker: the talk came to me after I had already written out a whole *other* talk, making me start from scratch just when I thought I was done! Frankly, it was very annoying. But this baby was scratching and clawing to come out and be heard—and it was *heard*. When the TEDx event day came, the organizer ended up making me the closing speaker, commenting as she announced me: "We saved the best for last."

And I *still* could not fully believe it. Impostor syndrome is a bitch!

After my talk, many young people with similar backgrounds and struggles—first-generation Americans born of immigrant parents—reached out to me to tell me how much my talk had touched them, acknowledged them, and sparked ideas! Someone actually *did* care about what I had to say! My words helped someone! I had found the advantage in my adversity.

Sometimes we are just paralyzed by fear.

*Sometimes our biggest roadblock*
*is our own fear*
*of our greatness.*

I see this often as a coach. A client, who I know is more than capable of holding their own, will say they don't feel ready enough or good enough or fill-in-the-blank enough. *Fear.* We let fear of the unknown set up mile-high roadblocks. Let me tell you something: You may *never* feel fill-in-the-blank enough. Many famously successful people admit they still don't.

### Mitch's Words of Wisdom:

**Failure is not the worst-case scenario.
The "what if?" is worse.**

It is better to go after an opportunity and fail, Fail Hard, than it is to wonder for the rest of your life, "What if?" The "what if" is the worst thing you will have to live with. When looking back on their lives, most people do not regret the things they did, but the things they did **not** do—the things left unsaid, the times they didn't fight back when they should have, the moment they failed to defend an ally. The time spent wondering about what the outcome *would* have been had they done things differently haunts more people than anything else.

As for me, some of my family members think I am

off-my-rocker, and always have been—a wild adventurer, unpredictable, a wanderer!

"When are you going to settle down?"

They don't even get that what they really mean is, "When are you going to stop dreaming? When are you going to stop following your intuition?" Or worse, "When are you going to stop being *you*, and just be *normal*?"

Normalcy is overrated, my friends.

Who of any great acclaim was ever thought of as *normal*? Can you name anyone?

Not everyone will understand or agree with your decisions or your vision. Who cares? What they may not understand is that you have what some of them do not—true fulfillment, honest happiness, and the peace of mind that comes from the certainty that you said, "*Si, por favor!*" to every opportunity, pass or fail, and can thankfully say you are not haunted by the "what if."

## CHAPTER 9

# How to Deal With Impostor Syndrome

**Have You Ever Felt like You Didn't *Deserve* to Be In the Room?**

IT WAS MY JUNIOR YEAR in a new high school. I had somehow made it past several auditions, despite having no training like some of my peers did, and found myself on stage as a lead in our school's production of *Cats*. Well, actually, they couldn't afford the royalties, so it was called *Junkyard Cats*, even though we were performing all of the songs from the Broadway show anyway.

As I stepped out on the stage with my partner for

the big duet, "Macavity!" I felt the sweat dripping down three layers of caked-on, do-it-yourself, cat makeup, my whole body trembled uncontrollably. I opened my mouth to belt out my part but a strange phenomenon occurred—my voice dropped. I don't mean it dropped in tone; it dropped on the floor, right in front of my feet! No one could hear me!

I panicked, tried to open my mouth wider and push my voice out my throat, yell it out if I had to, but the more I tried, the worse it got. I was clearly not in control. I was mortified! And as if that wasn't humiliating enough, my partner in the duet took over and started signing *my* part! I thought, *How dare she?* And then I thought, *I am definitely going to be kicked off this production. What gives me the right to be on this stage?*

I didn't know what I was doing and now every-body else knew it too.

I was new to the school, a junior in a senior produc-tion. I had no formal voice training, unless you count singing in church choirs and imitating rock singers.

My scene partner was also new to the school and even a year younger than me, a sophomore that had just transferred from LA. Yet she was light-years ahead of me in terms of vocal capacity, technique, and cool factor. Her dad was a movie producer; she had long, straight, blonde hair that carelessly draped over her face, wore skinny-tight rocker pants, a black leather jacket, and every official Broadway musical T-shirt available. I imagined she had a closet full of them, having been to every single one of them herself—the actual Broadway ones, not the traveling versions. She even had a cool name—*Dani* (later on, I wondered if the Red Hot Chili Peppers' song had been written about her). I hated her. She had *everything,* especially the one thing I desired most, musical training! I imagined she had a vocal coach from the time she was in the crib. Her voice was a sweet soprano, yet strong and piercing. When she auditioned, she brought the room to tears with her rendition of *Les Misérables*'s "On My Own." She even made the teachers cry! I hated her in that moment—but admittedly, I cried too.

I grew up poor. I didn't even know what *Les Mis* was until Dani came in, sporting the T-shirt with the little, crying girl. The only reason I knew *Cats* was because I remembered the commercials used to come on between my Saturday morning cartoons when I was a kid. I liked to think my voice teachers were Stevie Nicks, Robert Plant, and countless hair-band wailers. Boy, I could hit those notes on every Zeppelin song. My audition had no sheet music or accompaniment, I sang a mash-up of two rock ballads acapella. Out of my league!

What gave me the right to even audition? What made me think I could share the stage with *Dani California*? And most mysterious of all: How the heck did I *fool* them into picking me as a lead?!

I guess I did okay when I was in a room with my peers. But the moment I got out into the theater, jammed with wall-to-wall chairs full of students, jocks, faculty, and parents, I vocally froze up! And on opening night! I made a fool of myself, the production, and anyone who had agreed to let me onto that stage. I thought, *Well, this is the end for sure. My short-lived musical theater dream.*

The next day, I showed up at our little theater way before the rest of the class, dreading facing my teachers, ready for the chopping block.

Much to my dismay, Dani was already there. I was so embarrassed I couldn't even look her in the eye. I expected her to tell me what a loser I was and how I ruined her big number.

But she didn't.

Instead, she did something I didn't expect. She flashed me a very compassionate smile and kindly said, "You have an awesome voice." Now I was sure she was mocking me. "But if you don't get it out there"—she pointed to the back of the theater—"no one will ever know. Can I show you some techniques I use when I get nervous?"

*What?!* She *gets nervous?* The thought was preposterous.

The next thought was, *Why would she want to help me?*

And then, *tears.*

I was moved to tears. They were tears of relief, *somehow* she understood, that even *she* sometimes got nervous. Tears of shame, this girl I had been so busy hating was so eagerly willing to help me by sharing what she had been so privileged to learn. Privilege. There it was again. I did not have the privilege that she enjoyed, but that was okay. She was willing to *share* what she had learned in order to help me. Tears of hope and possibility.

"Okay, drop down and get on your back!"

She proceeded to teach me the basics of breathing and projecting. It was my first formal vocal coaching session. And the sessions would continue over the course of my junior year. And Dani became one of my best, lifelong friends.

The next night, I stepped out onto the stage with new confidence. I was still extremely nervous, but I was armed with something I did not have before—technique. It was not perfect, but I did manage to get my voice *out*, at least beyond my feet. And every performance thereafter was better and better. Thanks to Dani's patient coaching, we found

I *did* have a powerful voice and I learned how to wield it.

One year later, I brought our school the honorable *Superior* award from the theatrical state evaluations for my rendition of "I Dreamed a Dream" from *Les Miserables*—the same song that got me into NYU's Tisch School of the Arts.

## So, What Do You Do If You Don't Feel Fill-In-The-Blank Enough?

### 1. Do It Anyway

An opportunity may not present itself again, or at least not in the same way. Silence those inner and outer dream killers! Raise your hand and say, "*Si, por favor!*" (Yes, please!)

### 2. Get Busy Getting Wise

Lean on what you *do* know. Figure out what you *don't* know. Then, read everything you can about your knowledge gaps. Find mentors immediately that can help you by sharing what they have learned. Why reinvent the wheel when so many have traveled the road before you and are perfectly willing to hand you the map? Personally, I am a big fan of following a well-worn-in path. My ego doesn't dictate I always have to be the trailblazer.

When I was a green server, I would intently study the servers that made the most money, had the biggest sales, and the most regulars, to figure out what they were doing that I wasn't. What could I do better? I constantly listened in on their delivery, paid close attention to how they maneuvered and managed all the many moving parts, including the varied customer personalities. The desire to learn and to excel was my driving influence. I've never failed when applying myself this way. I leaned on what I did know, understood what I didn't, and got busy getting wise!

### 3.  Learn from Your Mistakes

You will make them, probably lots of them! Accept this fact and then learn what can be done better next time. Don't let your ego stand in the way of your development and growth. You have to be willing to let yourself be helped, be taught, be coached. I don't coach people who cannot introspect and identify their own shortcomings. People who cannot recognize their flaws cannot grow, do not learn, and are not coachable. That's why I always have a discovery coaching session *before* I take a client on. I need to ensure each person can be humble and honest with themselves enough to see where their opportunities lie. Only then can real and lasting shifts in point of view occur. This is what it takes to follow the road to wisdom. Mistakes will happen. If you can catch them quickly, understand fully why they were made, and what can be done better next time, *then* you can make progress. *Then* you will be making the most out of every opportunity.

**CHAPTER 10**

# The Singing Waitress

Remember: When Opportunity Comes to Your Door, You Must Raise Your Hand and Say, "*Si, Por Favor*!" (Yes, Please!)

AT THE END of my first semester at NYU, I learned that I had seriously misunderstood my financial-aid packet. What I thought covered me for a full year only covered me for one semester. I was crushed! Panicked! Where would I go? My familial relationships were extremely strained and complicated. Therefore, I did not really have a "home" to go back to.

I knew two things:

1. I was not leaving New York, and
2. I had to find a job where I could make a *lot* more money than my minimum-wage retail job.

A friend suggested that being a waitress was the best way to make a lot of cash quickly. I had no restaurant experience, but I was sure as heck going to figure out how to get into the restaurant industry!

As summer approached, I was quickly running out of time and would be homeless if I didn't find a place to live soon.

And then? Opportunity!

An opportunity came via my friend Silvio. He offered to share an apartment with me in the West Village. My initial response was, "Are you crazy?! I can't afford that!"

But Silvio came prepared. He handed me a *The Village Voice* newspaper with an ad circled in red:

"Wanted — Singing Waitress — Must audition to apply."

"Silvio," I argued, "I don't know anything about being a waitress!" I had applied to several restaurants as a greeter or a food runner—something to get my foot in the door and gain experience enough to move up to a server position in short time, I hoped.

Silvio was always keen on opportunities and very much a risk-taker. He was also pushy enough to make me act, despite my trepidations.

"Just blow them away with your singing and bullshit the rest!" I knew nothing about being a waitress, but I could sing!

So, despite my lack of experience and bogus résumé, I presented myself as a contender. Perhaps that is the fearlessness of youth, something we should all strive to hold onto as long as we can. Perhaps it was mere desperation. I was out of options if I wanted to keep my vision of living in NYC alive. Desperate optimism is apt fuel.

Audition day came. I was shaking with nerves, pretty sure they recognized this impostor posing as a waitress. The interviewing manager was a middle-aged, stout man who looked tired and jaded. His dream of directing shows on Broadway replaced by the reality that he was now directing dinner theater in a Jewish steakhouse. He intimidated the crap out of me! Who was I to think I could bullshit this guy?! I was quivering while trying to look confident. He eyed my résumé with one brow raised. I began to feel as if someone had turned on the heater and pointed it right at my face.

*He knows! Of course, he knows! How did I think this preposterous plan would work? Why did I listen to Silvio!*

I answered the interview questions as confidently, enthusiastically, and vaguely as I could. He did not seem impressed. He would half-acknowledge my answers with an "Mmhmm . . ."

"Alright, well, let's see what you got." He waved

his hand delicately toward the corner of the room, an open area of the dining room floor where an old, boney guy sporting a thick mustache and a cheap tux hung over a 1980s keyboard. I handed him my sheet music and took a deep breath before turning to face my judge.

This was my only shot. I was going to make the best of it—"*Si, por favor!*"

I controlled my quivering vocal cords and made my voice ring out through that restaurant with all the power in my eighteen-year-old lungs. The restaurant had not opened yet but the kitchen was being prepped for that evening's service. The cooks stopped what they were doing and came out of the kitchen to see who was attached to that voice. When I was done with my song, my long, curly hair was drenched in sweat, my hands were trembling with nervous adrenaline. I knew I had given it my all. That is all you can do when faced with an opportunity. Leave the rest up to God (or the universe, or karma, whatever you believe is out there guiding your journey).

Then, applause erupted—the cooks, the man on the keyboard, and even—yes!—the manager, who sighed deeply and said, "Okay, we'll give you a try."

I did it! I got my foot in the door! I leaned on what I knew. The rest of it I would have to learn quickly, hustle like my life depended on it—because it did!

Those first few months in the restaurant were absolutely terrifying! I got yelled at constantly by the angry Staten Island chef, "What are you, some kind of fackin' moron?!" I cried almost daily, lost some weight, lost some hair, lost a little bit of my sanity. But I persisted. I leaned in and I learned everything I could, as quickly as I could. I went from being a total mess, to not such a mess, to okay, to pretty good, to eventually being the one most called upon to train new servers.

One night after a long double shift that felt like surviving a war, about a year after I had started, the staff went out for drinks along with that manager. It was then that he admitted to me, in his huffiest tone, "Girrrl! I knew that résumé was a load of bull manure. I hired you because you could sing!"

That singing waitress job was the beginning of a long and lucrative career in hospitality for me. That also was the beginning of my life as an independent adult, living at the heart of the West Village in New York City!

**When opportunity comes to your door,**
**you must raise your hand and say,**
*"Si, por favor!"*

## CHAPTER 11

# Why We Self-Sabotage

ROADBLOCKS CAN COME unexpectedly and from many different directions. Perhaps the most insidious of them all is the one that comes from the closest source—ourselves!

Why do we stop ourselves from succeeding? We talked about why we shy away from opportunity, but what about when we are in *it*—in the job, in the relationship, living the dream, or close enough to reach the horizon, and we sabotage ourselves from reaching it? Why do we do that? Like impostor syndrome, there are many reasons. However, in my coaching and life experience I have observed two main reasons that are real doozies:

1.  **We Believe What We Receive, and**

2.  **Fear of the Unknown (or the Uncontrollables)**

Let me expand on these and offer some remedies for each as well.

## 1.   We Believe What We Receive

Just like the saying, "We achieve what we believe we can achieve," we also tend to believe what we *receive*. From the time we are born, we are bombarded by messages, points of view, false ideas, and limiting beliefs. We receive these and soak them in as truth, letting them shape our views, what we think we want, and who we believe we are. We receive them from all sorts of sources—parents, teachers, friends, TV, and social media. We are shaped by these messages we receive every waking hour. Sometimes we see them for what they are—preposterous. But other times we absorb them right into our core, like a virus, without realizing they are slowly killing our spirit.

When I was a little girl, I heard this saying a lot among my Cuban family in relation to my propensity to speak my mind, *"Los niños hablan cuando las gallinas mean!"* (Kids speak when chickens pee!)

Some of you may be laughing in familiarity right now. I didn't get it. I didn't grow up around chickens much. My grandfather would chuckle at my baffled face and explain. "Don't you see? Chickens don't pee!"

Luckily, I was naturally too boisterous and extroverted to let that stop me from speaking, earning me many scoldings and beatings as a result. However, not everyone is so impervious to this kind of molding. Some of the clients I coach specifically on public speaking are so stuck in that "children should be seen and not heard" mold from their childhood, that as adults they struggle with verbal expression or group communication. That is the power of words—words from outside, and the words we tell ourselves as a result.

We believe what we receive.

How does that then play into self-sabotage? We *act* on the beliefs we absorb from the messages we repeatedly receive. If we constantly hear "all is doom and gloom!" from media, friends, family, etc. we start to become depressed, apathetic, and ultimately stop reaching for our dreams, because: "What's the point?"

If you hear enough times that you are stupid, you start believing it. If you hear how ugly you are (Yes, people! Some family members are *that* cruel), you may see yourself as ugly and unlovable to the extent of sabotaging good relationships, because: "What's the point? Eventually, they will see me for what I really am—*ugly*."

Conversely, people who are constantly told, since childhood, that their actions have *no* consequences and that they are entitled to take anything they want become megalomaniacs. Can you think of a few examples of this?

The messages we receive—really receive, absorb into our minds, and accept as truth—have an impact on our actions and behaviors, even if subconsciously.

The good news is that this works on the positive as well. You can choose the messages you hear and the sources that surround you. If you surround yourself with people who are succeeding, contributing to society, upbeat, and exuding positive messages, you will soak that in as well. If your circle of friends and colleagues are supportive and reassuring, you will eventually feel like maybe they have a point! Maybe you *do* deserve to succeed. This is why choosing your connections is so vital to your success and to attaining your seemingly impossible dreams. I know people who are very smart and capable, but who stay in miserable dead-end jobs because they have family members all around them who constantly tell them that their vision is childish, unrealistic, and a waste. "When are you going to grow up and get real?"

So even if a prime opportunity does present itself, they shy away from it, seeing the concerned faces of those family members. Sadly, sometimes even family can be a weight on your neck in the ocean of life, where you are flapping your arms and legs as hard as you can to swim for the horizon, let alone just to stay afloat.

**The Remedy**

So, what is the remedy?

Well, if the damage has been ingrained in you enough from childhood, you may need a good therapist just to unpack some of that baggage. If you are receiving the negative, soul-crushing, and counterproductive messages currently, then it is time to bite the bullet and go on what I like to call a Negative Sources Diet! This is something I recommend to my clients who are feeling overwhelmed by all the negative news, be it on social media or news channels.

**Negative Sources Diet**

1. Take inventory of what messages are being piped through to you daily.

2. Ask yourself, "Does this source of messaging invigorate, energize, and inspire me, or does it drain me, belittle me, or make me feel like I can't, shouldn't, couldn't reach for my goals?

3. Cut out the negative sources: news, social media, toxic people (yes, even family members)

who are throwing shade on your dreams. Take a break (for some sources, you may have to make it a permanent one).

## Surround Yourself with What You Want

Actively surround yourself with sources of positive, productive, useful, and inspiring messages. You can find that in books, podcasts, professional organizations, or by just making friends with people who inspire you—and kick your butt a little, too.

You can also find inspiration on social media. I don't agree that social media is a monster that devours everyone's soul. It can do that if you are too obsessive, but if you schedule out some time to follow people that are either doing what you strive to do, succeeding despite adversity, or sharing positive and thought-provoking messages, then you are finding true advantage in that medium. I slice in some time daily to read posts and watch videos from people I admire or strive to be more like.

The point is that you get what you focus on. If your focus is sucked into negativity and the people who dole it out, that is what your life will be full of. If your focus is on books, videos, people, friends, family, and groups that deal in positivity and possibilities, then that is what you will get.

There are definitely people I have either cut out

completely or cut down to very small and infrequent doses of contact with because, at one time, they were sucking away my energy by involving me in constant drama. I would feel dizzy in the head and sickened after just a few minutes of conversation with them. So, I had to decide—victim or victor? In this case, being the victor meant taking control of my own life, my desired energy, and the types of communications I chose to allow into my space. These were hard decisions. It will not be easy to break ties from some of those sources that you habitually have leaned on or allowed to lean on you. However, the adverse effect of keeping these in your life is your own misery. Again, victim or victor—you are the source ultimately of your own happiness and success. Stop putting up that roadblock.

## 2. Fear of the Unknown (or the Uncontrollables)

I once knew a lady who constantly broke up with good boyfriends just when it seemed to be getting serious because she would rather be in control and break it off than be the one broken up with. Now, some of these men were not ideal matches, but there were one or two who seemed promising, and yet she was so terrified of failing that she would cut out before the going even got tough. She really did dream of marriage and children and that white picket fence (well, that last one I may have thrown in for good measure), but she just didn't believe she could achieve that.

Fear is a perception.

Many people will quit an endeavor just as they are reaching the horizon, only because they are too afraid of the unknown, the uncontrollables—what they cannot predict and prepare for. People leave dream jobs just as they are about to land the big promotion or quit a business just as it's about to skyrocket because somehow it seems easier to go the safe route than to take a risk. By the way, this "safe route" equals personal misery. Just like I hate drama, I hate misery! Why would anyone choose that?! Because the fear of the unknown *seems* bigger than the road yet to be traveled.

**The Remedy**

1.  Surround yourself with people who are succeeding so that you may see that the path before you *is* real, and the possibility that it *can* be done. This may mean joining a professional organization, following successful people on social media, hiring a coach, or joining a mastermind group (this is a group of peers who come together to share professional ideas, best practices, motivation, accountability, and resources). You get what you

focus on, so put the focus on how you *can* do it and not on all the reasons why you think you can't.

2. When terrified, do it anyway! Do it and keep at it with the thought that you are doing everything you can so that you will have No Regrets. Remember:

**Failure is not the worst-case scenario.**
**The "What If" is!**

3. Vision! Remember the rule:

**Roadblocks (even self-imposed) =**
**Circle back to the vision!**

4. Reread chapter two when you feel like you are losing sight of that vision.

## CHAPTER 12

# Faking It?

IN THE LATE '90S, after years of suffering through the winters in New York, longing to be near the ocean again, to take midnight bike rides on the boardwalk and morning runs along the shore, I moved back to Florida. I had no money saved and living with my family was not an option. So instead, I crashed with my best friend who had a tiny studio apartment in South Beach. I was grateful to be sharing that tiny space. I had left NYC for sunny Miami, leaving behind my first long-term serious relationship, looking to start fresh and figure out my next step in life.

Now I just needed to make enough money to afford my own little place. I was working for an upscale restaurant, but I was not making enough to afford South Beach living. Then one night, I was hanging out at a bar with some friends, and one of them introduced me to a handsome, snazzy-dressed young man.

He said, "Mike here is a baller! He makes a killing bartending at one of the hottest spots on South Beach. The staff dance on the bar!"

*OOH! This sounds intriguing*, I thought.

Mike humbly smiled and said, "I do all right."

I began drilling him with a barrage of questions—average a bartender could make a night there? (It was a *lot*—an executive salary at minimum.) What kind of dancing? (Latin music mostly—salsa, merengue, samba—I did not know samba, my salsa was not great, but I could surely rock a merengue!) And the most important question, how could I get a shot?

"Can you dance? If you can dance, that beats bartending experience every time," he said with a disapproving shake of his head.

"I can dance!" (Hey, I was a singing waitress with no prior waitressing experience. This time I had some—very minimal—bartending experience. At least I knew I could pick up a drink book and memorize every recipe in there if I had an opportunity. But dancing? I could do that!)

"I can put in a good word for you. Can't promise

more than an interview, but they are always looking." A testament to the kindness of strangers, he was so sweet to have just met me and still be willing to extend that offer, an offer I, of course, raised my hand for—"*Si, por favor!*"

I went into the interview with swagger, like I knew all there was to know about the world of cocktails. The manager looked me over as if assessing a show dog. He asked a bit about my experience and more about my knowledge of the Latin and Caribbean dances. I said, "I'm a Cuban from Miami—what do you think?" Not a direct answer and not a lie. I figured, like drink recipes, I would learn what dances I needed as I went along.

Sometimes you have to take the plunge and have faith in yourself, in your ability and desire to soak in whatever you need to make it. Here is where courage and faith come in. The famous phrase "fake it until you make it" is famous for some reason. But it is not entirely true.

**You can't fake your way through everything.**

You can't fake an engineering job or accounting if you have no knowledge or skill in those areas. You can't totally fake dancing or bartending either. You have to have a base from which to start, an entry point. You have to know something about what you are endeavoring to do, even if it is just theoretical—from books, observing, asking questions. The rest can only come from *doing*. I am not suggesting you allege you are an expert in something you've never done before. But don't be afraid to say, "I know something about that and am willing to learn and become an expert as quickly as possible." That goes a long way, even for bosses.

In the case of my waitressing experience, I did go in completely blind and dumb. I had never done it before, and it was impossible to take a job like that with no experience whatsoever. Impossible! So, I did the impossible *that* time. I got lucky. Sometimes desperation makes us brave and grants us ingenuity. In that case, I still had something that was of value to the company—my singing skills. That was worth overlooking my lack of service skills, they needed a great show. They took a risk with me and I think I provided sufficient reward, I hustled, I learned quickly. I took my mistakes personally and swore not to repeat them. And I gave them a great show every time. It worked out for all involved, win-win.

It may not always work out—the leap, the "fake," the attempt to do something when you don't know for certain you'll succeed. Many of the great people in history who did succeed took this chance; many of them also failed multiple times before "making it."

*You* may fail. However, don't be afraid to fail big! Fall on your face and know, deep in your soul, this path you tried out is absolutely not for you. How can you tell for sure if you don't fail big? How could you know?

In the case of the bartending gig, I landed it. I was a little too curvy for the tight animal print outfits and not a great dancer at first. This meant I got the worst shifts in the worst bars (there were multiple bars within the venue). However, I got many shifts because I was coming in fresh, not burnt out yet like the others, and the only thing I was focused on at that time was my job. So, I worked a lot. Long hours, many days in a row—in at six p.m., out around five a.m., just in time to get breakfast at the diner before going to bed. I attended the weekly, mandatory dance classes and vowed to *get great fast*.

I practiced at home in front of mirrors. I started to improve—and so did my bar shifts. The main bar was the big goal. Only the girls with the biggest chests, in the tightest outfits, with the sexiest dance moves got there. They were making **bank**! All the male bartenders contended to work alongside them, as each bar shared their bank. It was only fair. While the ladies did most of the heavy lifting with the dance numbers, the men had to hustle that much more to push out the mojitos, frozen fruity slushies, and Sex on the Beaches.

In a matter of months, I made it from the upstairs hidden bar to the back of the joint overflow bar to the front side bar. It was the second-best bar, a hectic and lucrative station, quite a financial jump—but it still was not far enough. Learning more and more dance moves and getting signature dance numbers aided in my ascension to the second-best bar. Yet I was still not satisfied. My eye was on the main bar.

Finally, after a year of honing my skills both at dancing and making ten mojitos at breakneck speed, despite not having the huge implants most main-bar chicks had, I got there—some shifts each week— enough to make me feel I had succeeded. Then came the additional benefits from that exposure. I started getting offers as a professional dancer—a national commercial for the top credit card company, a dance spot at Miami's famous Calle Ocho festival, samba festivals, and even a trip to New York to appear at S.O.B.'s—the famous Latin jazz club—as the featured flamenco dancer for a Gypsy Kings-offshoot band!

All those late nights, dance classes, nasty protein bars and shakes, near-starvation diets, fat burners, and complete lack of social life (I was sleeping and working when most people were gathering) paid . . . off?

I wish I would have been taught at an early age how to manage money. Unfortunately, the American

mis-education system did not prepare me for finan-
cial success in life, did not teach me about smart
money management. Maybe it's on purpose, all those
credit card offers once you turn eighteen, with no clue
how the system works, so that you are eventually a
slave to the monetary system. Maybe that is the way
the economic game is structured—get them mired
in debt as early as possible to keep the American-
banking machine going. While I am not a financial
advisor—I have one that has been instrumental in
helping me not only get out of debt but grow multiple
investment funds—I do often help my coaching cli-
ents who are mired in debt with some helpful sugges-
tions—books, tools, and simple strategies—point
them in the right direction until they can really afford
to work with a financial advisor. Debt is a common
roadblock to success. If you have to work to support
paying off debt, it is difficult to focus on anything else
sometimes. I have been there for the greater part of
my life. Yet it is a roadblock I could have gotten a han-
dle on in my early twenties, had I been given the right
guidance.

At the ripe age of twenty-five, I was already in a
ton of debt from credit cards and student loans, debt
I had accumulated prior to this bartending job. With
the money I made at this bar, I could have paid off
all my student loans and credit card debts, saved for

retirement, and invested in a South Beach condo that would be worth a fortune now! Some of my fellow bartenders did just that. Why didn't I take a cue from them? I was making so much cash, banking it in chunks weekly, that one night, as I was heading out with friends, I grabbed a jacket that I hadn't worn in weeks (in Miami, opportunities to wear jackets are few and far between) and reached into a pocket to discover a wad of cash amounting to about $300 I had somehow *forgotten* about, forgotten to deposit! Instead of investing in my future, I invested in friends, cars, and clothing, all of which are no longer around. Instead of diligently paying off all debts, I carried those debts with me and compounded them for almost twenty more years! If only I had read Dave Ramsey back then! Financial literacy should be a continuous, major subject in school.

I was twenty-five and I was making more than an executive salary in a bar—*in cash*!

I was also tired, lonely, jumpy from the fat burners (which were later taken off the market), in debt, and mostly miserable.

Sometimes you have to succeed big—"make it"—to know you are definitely *not* where you want to be. And that is totally OK! That is just as fruitful and valuable as the failure track. Life is so funny. We win big—we learn. We lose big—we learn. I guess the point is not whether we win or lose, but learning what truly brings you happiness. If you learn that, you have cracked the code to real success.

## Opportunity Exercise

What opportunities have you missed, not taken, or shied away from? Think of any opportunities in the past or any you may be contemplating at this moment.

1.  Write down what makes you shy away from the opportunity (all the "not fill-in-the-blank enough" reasons).
2.  Write down what could happen if you pursued the opportunity and failed. What's the worst-case scenario?
3.  Now write down what could happen if you took the opportunity and succeeded. What's the best-case scenario?
4.  List all the things you could do to get fill-in-the-blank enough to succeed.
5.  Get busy!

# PART THREE

# Lean On
# Your Resources

**CHAPTER 13**

# Lean On Your Resources

MUCH LIKE OPPORTUNITIES, you are surrounded by resources, but sometimes you don't recognize them. Sometimes, you don't feel you deserve to ask, or you're afraid to lean on those resources. Additionally, sometimes we misunderstand what resources really are. Often when working with clients who need help with a huge life transition, I will have them work on a list of their resources. Funny enough, the list always starts off really small because they have a limited idea of what a resource *is*.

When I get them to understand the full definition and invite them to dig deeper? Jackpot!

Suddenly, they discover that they actually have a wealth of resources!

Many people have a limited view, which makes them feel like they have no resources at all. I promise you there is an abundance of resources all around you, all the time. You may simply have gone blind to them. Let us illuminate these underutilized gems.

Oxford Languages defines a resource as "a stock or supply of money, materials, staff, and other assets that can be drawn on by a person or organization in order to function effectively." It also defines it as "an action or strategy which may be adopted in adverse circumstances."

I want to widen your concept of what a resource is for *you*; get you looking beyond what's in your bank account and what obvious physical assets you have. You may read this and think, "But I have no money and no assets!" I challenge you to dig deeper.

Resources can be friends, family, contacts, but they are also your experiences, your skills, the things you have learned along the way that are somehow applicable today. Resources come in many different forms. And when roadblocks appear, a resource can be "an action or strategy which may be adopted in adverse circumstances."

When I invite my coaching clients to write down a list of resources, I then ask some meaningful coaching questions. I get them to look beyond the bank sheets, the classes they took, or the title on their diploma. What skills have you learned along the way that are *not* on a certificate?

Perhaps, for example, you were a bartender for years and now are looking to move into a corporate sales position, but you feel like you are not qualified. Do you know what kind of salesmanship it takes in order to thrive in the service industry? Only the best salespeople get the best shifts. You may not have taken an official sales class, but if you have been doing it for years—and doing well—I would venture you can teach others a thing or two. You have to highlight your experiences and provide statistics, like how much revenue you generated for that bar or restaurant. *Show* how your sales skills impacted that company.

What about the skills that are grossly misnamed "soft skills"? If handling difficult people is a "*soft* skill," whoever came up with that term has never worked in customer service a day in their lives! If you worked in customer service, hospitality, or real estate, you have worked with people, dealt with different personalities, and handled conflicts. If you performed well, you have developed important transferable skills. These skills are the make-or-break of any great leader, salesperson, or parent even!

What have you mastered along the way? These are resources to lean on. They will inform the "action or strategy which may be adopted in adverse circumstances."

I invite you to sit down and think about this deeply. Write out your list of resources. Keep it updated. You never know when roadblocks will pop up and you will need to have this list handy so you can then execute the L in VOLAR: **Lean On Your Resources**!

My husband worked as a sales and service manager for the Tampa Bay Lightning professional hockey organization. When looking for a new sales representative, they often received applicants who, like himself, had a sports administration master's degree or had been interning and working in some sports organization previously. Many of these candidates would get the jobs, but one time they hired someone whose skill set and experience was a little different, someone who instead of previously working for a professional team had worked in a restaurant for years.

Now you may ask, "A restaurant? What does that have to do with working for a sports team?" And that guy could have asked himself the same thing and refrained from even *trying* for his dream job. Luckily, he knew exactly how his skills could transfer and the hiring managers also understood. They knew that this person could be taught the sports and team aspect, but salesmanship and handling high volumes of people in the restaurant industry? *That* is the experience that got him his first job working for a major pro sports franchise.

That guy could have said to himself, "Nah! They will never consider me." He could have talked himself out of leaning on those resources, the skills he had acquired along the way. Instead, he took a chance. And the team took a chance on him. As a result, he was able to live his dream of working in pro sports. What's even more exciting? In 2020 and 2021, as part of the administrative staff, he got an even bigger dream come true: TWO championship rings from the back-to-back Tampa Bay Lightning Stanley Cup victories! (Unfortunately, having left just a short time prior to the first of the repeat wins, my husband got ZERO rings, a fact I may still be a tiny bit saucy over.)

It takes a leap of faith and a willingness to lean—and sometimes lean **hard**—on your resources.

Remember that vision I had to move from New Jersey to LA within three months with no money?

During that recon trip to LA, I got the opportunity to meet with my old friend, Silvio. He was so excited to have me in LA that he hosted a dinner party in my honor. I took the opportunity to proudly present him my CD since he had always been so supportive of my music. In high school, he would make me take my guitar to parties so he could gather the hippie kids to sit around and hear me sing. He was one of my oldest friends, and he turned out to be an amazing resource as well.

The day after the dinner, Silvio gave my CD to the music manager of *Ugly Betty*. The next thing I knew I was sitting in a big, posh office in Beverly Hills meeting with this guy! I felt intensely nervous as he entered the room and sat before me, his desk strewn with all kinds of CDs, some with band names I recognized and loved! The feeling overwhelmed me. *What the hell am I doing here?* (Impostor syndrome is a bitch!)

The music manager smiled and held up my CD. "This is good stuff."

I thought, *No way!*

Then he asked the killer question, "Do you have anything in Spanish?"

Ugh! At that point, I heard my Cuban mother's voice in my head, "I told you, you should write more songs in Spanish! Why don't you have more songs in Spanish?" Boy, I hate it when my mother is right!

I did have *one* song in Spanish, but it wasn't even fully recorded yet. What do we say when opportunity comes to our door?

"Yes, I do, but . . . it's . . . not quite finished yet."

"Great!" he replied. "We have an episode coming up that needs a Spanish song. When can you finish and send it to me?"

"The first week of December?" (It was the second week of November. Was I crazy?)

He gave me a firm handshake and an enthusiastic smile. "Great! No promises, but I look forward to hearing it."

Well, I had my vision, I had an amazing opportunity, and now it was time to go back to Jersey and lean on some resources. I had tapped out my finances putting out my CD, so I called my friend Gordon. He agreed, out of the kindness of his heart, to record my song in his studio. By "studio," I mean it was basically a studio *apartment*—with a couch and some recording equipment in it. But hey! It did the trick. In a matter of a few days, we recorded something that I felt really good about, good enough to submit to *Ugly Betty*. I sent the song, as promised, by the first week in December!

**Lean on your resources.**

## Exercise

I have my coaching clients put a good deal of time and thought into listing out *all* their resources. Now, I invite you to do the same.

List everything that comes to mind. Put the list down for a little while, come back to it, and then list out some more. When you think you are done, great! Write some more.

You don't have to wait until you are facing a major roadblock to make this list. It is actually a good thing to do periodically—update it regularly and keep it in a file somewhere. You never know when you are going to have to pull this thing out and use it.

## CHAPTER 14

# Faith and Humility

ASIDE FROM UNDERSTANDING what your resources are, you need two more things in order to fully utilize this VOLAR step—*faith* and *humility*.

### Faith

You need faith in your ability to actually **lean** in and make full use of your skills, your abilities, and the things you have learned along the way. You need faith in yourself to believe that you really have learned these things and can put them to use. You also need faith in the resources and friends that will come to your aid if you need them.

When I took that South Beach bartending job in

my early twenties, I had studied a lot about mixology and watched the bartenders I had worked with for years to get an understanding of what made them successful. When it came time to put what I had learned into practice—something I honestly had a limited amount of—I had to lean in and trust that I would probably make some (or tons) of mistakes, but that I had a basic foundation and was smart enough to figure it out and get better fast!

Leaning on resources also takes faith in those resources and in what you will do with them.

## Humility

Humility is probably the toughest element to tackle. You need the humility required to be open and vulnerable and say, "I need help!"

I find that women, especially, can sometimes struggle with this, feeling like we must uphold our superwoman image: balancing babies, businesses, and baking while keeping our makeup intact and our heels unbroken. Perhaps this is changing more and more as women take on more leadership roles worldwide, but there is still this sense of pride we carry. Perhaps it is what makes us so resilient in the face of adversity. However, pride can be a major roadblock in itself. We don't want to burden anyone with our problems and don't want to say "no" when we have overextended ourselves. One year, I found myself juggling so many committees and board responsibilities across various professional organizations that I felt as if I was drowning! I couldn't let anyone down or admit that I had accepted more than I could digest and was headed for deadly heartburn.

It was then that I learned a very important lesson about pride, self-care, and saying "no" more often. It is a lesson I share with all my clients, especially women. I learned that it's more important, and more productive in the long run, to say "no" first, or say "Let me think about it and circle back. I don't want to make a promise or take on a commitment that I cannot fully make good on at this time." Say "NO!" or buy yourself some time to really consider what is being asked of you, what time commitment will be expected, and how will you balance it with all your other responsibilities. Put the pride aside and admit when you just have too much going on to take on one more thing. To take it a step further, learn to delegate more.

In the case of needing help, be willing to put the pride aside and say, "I need help!"

This was not easy for me, especially when it came to money, having grown up with my mother's annoyed response to anything I ever asked for—"*No hay dinero!*" (There is no money!) When I found myself having to ask for financial help, even knowing that I would pay back my debts, it produced a nauseous feeling. I would rather have danced on tabletops for money than *ask* for a loan, even from my father. It felt like the most demeaning position. Yet if I had not asked for help in times when I needed it, I may still be homeless today. (Probably not, I am pretty crafty, but it would have been a much tougher climb, for sure.)

This feeling also permeated my ability to ask for a raise, even when I knew I deserved it! My mother's voice would ring in my head—"*No hay dinero!*" The altruist in me would feel guilty for even considering the question, with so many people struggling since the world is *obviously* out of resources! Oh, the roadblocks we impose on ourselves!

Here is a powerful affirmation:

The world is **not** devoid of resources. It is abundant! There is a **lot** of money out there. While some people may be hoarding it greedily, if you had all that money, you would contribute! What would you contribute? Think about that. Visualize it. Tell yourself that you are worthy, deserving, and responsible enough to amass wealth and share that wealth!

After a keynote I delivered on this topic, someone

in the audience asked, "But what if I have *no* resources?"

To that, I replied, "Dig deeper. You have them. You just aren't recognizing them or perhaps you just haven't turned over every rock yet."

The exercise at the end of this section on resources will help you in your investigatory stage. You can also work with a coach as a powerful resource, even if through a few very focused sessions. Sometimes it takes a coaching conversation to shed light on answers you don't immediately see.

Another audience member asked, "How do you go about asking for help?"

To this I offer, especially when making a financial ask, be very clear and specific about what exactly you are asking for, and then have a realistic, well-prepared plan as part of the ask. If you are going to ask for a loan, for example, lay out your repayment terms, how and when you will pay it back. When people see you have a plan, they are more confident in lending a financial hand.

Once when I was very young, I asked a friend for a loan. It took me years to pay her back and I always felt like a criminal, ashamed in her presence, constantly avoiding her, which is very sad because today (after I got control of my finances and paid her back in full) she is one of my oldest and dearest friends. Any time after, when I borrowed money, I laid out exactly how I planned to repay it and made sure to do so in less time than promised. Today, I carry zero debts. Today, I understand that wealth is not a mystical thing only available to the few that are lucky enough to be born into it.

Do not let your past traumas and false prophecies about money—*"No hay dinero!"*—color your view and block you from creating your wealth. You are smart enough and capable enough of achieving what you set out to. You will work for it, create for it, and then contribute to others with it. It is not a question of whether you *deserve* to make money; it is a question of the world *needing* you and all your full potential of resources (including money) to help make a positive impact.

Go forth with *faith* and *humility*. Go change your world.

## CHAPTER 15

# Contribution Begets Contribution

ALL THE STEPS and strategies to achieving and succeeding would do you no good without one integral component—contribution.

You can be focused, work hard, clarify your vision until it leaps off the page at you, but still fall short if you fail to fully grasp this one important thing: you get what you give.

<u>Mitch's Words of Wisdom:</u>
The more you seek ways to contribute, the more resources will rise to back you up when you need it most.

All along my career, my advancements hinged on the fact that I always looked for ways to be of service. If I was working as a server, I learned quickly that the greedy and selfish servers often had a hard time getting the rest of the team to help them out when in need. The more amiable and helpful ones? Well, people just couldn't say "no" to a call for help from them. I learned that the more I stepped beyond my own duties and found ways to stretch and offer assistance to those around me and above me, the more valuable I became. Along with that came promotions and goodwill.

When I was first getting certified as a professional coach, I offered my skills to my HR department at the company I worked for. I coached employees who were directly reporting to me and others in my department, and I delivered workshops for the whole staff, though it was outside of my job responsibilities. I was making myself valuable by contributing what I could to the bigger team.

How do you contribute outside your immediate sphere of influence right now? How could you contribute more?

Even when you are starting off with establishing your vision, you will enhance your scope if you include this one question:

"How will attaining my vision enable me to contribute to others?"

This is the question that also helps us overcome the self-sabotaging ideas of unworthiness or fear of reaching too high. We will reach higher and stretch ourselves more sometimes if we are stretching for the benefit of another over ourselves. Even in amassing wealth, some people have a hard time with the subject of money and cannot visualize themselves building wealth. This is especially rough for people who have struggled with poverty early on like myself—my mother's voice in my head, constantly affirming *"No hay dinero!"*

Then you grow up and still struggle to get that voice and self-fulfilling affirmation out of your head! Been there!

What helped me get past it? The idea of contribution, the hope that someday I would be affluent enough for philanthropy. To some, the concept of amassing wealth for the sake of wealth is unpalatable. When you stretch that horizon and consider how many ways you can contribute with that wealth— who would you donate money to, what would having wealth free up your time to contribute more to, how would that wealth help your community or nonprofits you are passionate about—now we are cooking! Now we can look beyond the negative connotations we may have on the subject of money because we have shifted focus to a greater purpose!

That's not to say there aren't plenty of greedy and unscrupulous people that comprise part of the world's tiny percent of economic power. But if you look at building economic power as a way to tilt the scale and make that power more productive for the whole planet, you will have no excuse as to why *you* shouldn't be one in that tiny percent! Look beyond the money, just as when you are pushing a vision to a team. What does the money *mean*? What problems will it solve for you, your family, your groups, your community, your world? How much more can you contribute if you attain your vision?

It works for our personal health and wellness goals as well. Sometimes we will let even our health go to crap, despite the urgency to change, until it affects the ones we love or care about.

A friend of mine was suffering from all kinds of health issues, mostly related to her obesity. She knew that her weight was a dangerous factor in her ailments and that if she did not do something to lose weight and get healthy, she'd probably die at an incredibly young age. This probability made her reach for a weight loss goal, the vision being so clear it was striking her in the face daily—being healthy, staying alive to watch her kids grow. Still, she would start a diet and quickly revert to her bad habits of fast food, rich and starchy meals, with no exercise in sight. To make matters worse, her teenage daughter was eating like she was. Kids! Who cares what they eat, right?

My friend struggled with the diet yo-yos until one day, her daughter was diagnosed with dangerously high cholesterol, which was causing other urgent health issues. Finally, her wake-up call! She completely changed her whole dietary strategy, learned how to cook healthy recipes, and started taking daily walks with her daughter.

Sometimes we will stretch more for others than we will for ourselves. It's kind of a beautiful testament of humans' innate goodness and desire to help.

Sometimes, a client will have a goal that seems aggressive and will find it hard to get motivated until I invite them to dig into what that attainment will mean for their whole team. When I get them to focus on others, something interesting happens. Suddenly, they feel more motivated to succeed! Envisioning the whole team's success is more inspiring than their own personal achievement.

Remember—part of focusing on vision is to keep this vital piece in mind: what will that vision contribute to your family, your groups, and the world at large? Everyone can think of at least something they want to contribute, even if it is just money in their kids' bank account. Find the contribution factor and you will find the motivation and a wealth of resources to lean on!

## CHAPTER 16

# How to Inspire Cooperation

IF YOU ARE TRYING to gain cooperation from a group, attain new clients, or grow your business, the amount of energy you offer toward contributing something of value will bring you the growth you desire through the number of contributions that will flow your way. It is like a universal law—the energy you put out will come back to you in some way.

In business, I will regularly check in with my contacts, offer a helpful article or short video to handle some issue they or their team is facing, and those same customers will often come back with a referral or an opportunity! I'll go to a networking event and focus on connecting some of my colleagues with people I feel will help them in their efforts, making myself a resource to them with no strings attached. Do you know what happens as a result? I gain goodwill and support, as those people want to find ways to reciprocate, and often do. Or I'll be on the phone with a colleague, just offering tips and tools to help them in their business with no expectations, just a true desire to be helpful, and they'll, in turn, offer something unexpectedly helpful to me like a connection to a lucrative speaking or coaching opportunity. Just another testament to the true goodness of people—if you honestly help them, they will want to do something to give back in return! You get what you give, even if it is not always in the way you expect.

I couldn't drill in this concept enough when I was directing new managers in the hospitality industry. I would repeatedly remind them, "If you honestly show your team that you are here to help them—help them get through the shift, help them make money, help them grow—then they will go to war for you!"

Living out this philosophy as a restaurant manager meant I was often in an expensive suit, bending down to pick up heavy, overloaded bus tubs so my bartenders could focus on the clients in front of them, thereby increasing their tips and decreasing their stress levels. Those bartenders would, in turn, cover any shift I needed help with. What wouldn't they do to help "Mama Mitch"?

It seems like such a simple concept, yet so many bosses fail to grasp it! If you take care of your staff, they will bend over backward to take care of you when you need them. We are talking resources here—human resources. People will quit jobs and make a lateral move, or even take a pay cut, just to go where they feel more valued, where they feel like they are truly contributing.

I once worked for a boss who firmly believed that if he told anyone they were doing a good job, they would stop producing as well, getting complacent and lazy. That belief told me how he viewed others and the world around him. He was one of the most mentally abusive bosses I ever worked under, leading me to quit a company I had been very loyal to for over a decade! He did nothing to support, grow, or validate me—never giving any indication that I would ever get promoted . . . until the day I gave my notice.

"Oh," he grunted, "and I was just going to promote you. I think you're making a big mistake leaving."

All that time I had slavishly worked under him with no feedback, no coaching, not a word of positive reinforcement or, if there were any, they were quickly followed by a big "BUT . . ." and a list of all the ways in which I sucked. All the anxiety and sobs on the way to work, for him to—at the moment of my departure—tell me I was actually valued and that I needed to stay? I remained composed, hoping my naturally expressive face wouldn't give away my disgust, and graciously replied, "I appreciate that, but my decision is made."

I had worked for that company for over ten years and would have continued to do so had it not been for my nightmarish experience working under this one horrible boss.

Sadly, so many companies lose out on valuable human resources due to lack of training, coaching, motivating, and validating—many times as a result of making new managers lead teams with no experience and no coaching. New and self-involved or old, terrible, and unchecked executives will push more good staff off the team than clumsy-but-caring managers. People will take less money and contribute happily if they absolutely love the boss they work for, knowing how hard such an environment has historically been to find.

Remember: contribution begets contribution.

The effort you put into lifting others up will ultimately grease the wheels of your train to success!

Partners, clients, and friends will come to your

aid, support you in your endeavors, and fill directional wind beneath your wings if you just make yourself helpful! Be of value. Look for ways to contribute to those around you, and you will find no shortage of resources or contribution to your efforts toward your ultimate vision!

**CHAPTER 17**

# Beware of Vampires

BEWARE OF VAMPIRES! I am not talking about the *True Blood*, sexy types, nor the type Buffy slays in her show—the type with fangs and mystical powers.

I'm talking about your very real and very danger-ous emotional vampires. Be wary of the vampire per-sonalities that will suddenly show up in the guise of an overly needy or intensely supportive friend, lover, or group. They may be different than the Hollywood version, but they are just as bloodthirsty. No matter if you are at a low point or a very high point, both situations can be perfect moments of opportunity for these creatures. They show up when you least expect and when you think you need them most. They may seemingly offer great opportunity or resources, but they will never actually lead to anything but loss—loss of identity, money, credibility, faith in yourself or your abilities, family, true friends. Most importantly, they will cost you time—the one thing you cannot get more of.

I find it imperative, as we talk about contribution and giving, to also include this giant warning sign here.

At twenty-five, the dancing bartender was lost, far from knowing what made her happy. It's in this state of mind that people, especially young people, tend to slip into the fangs of vampires. These manipulative souls have a keen eye for people at their lowest, severely suffering from a deep lack of self-esteem, and manage to attach themselves like leeches. They attack your self-reliance in insidious ways. They may start by lifting you up, affirming how great you are, how beautiful, how talented, and claiming to be your best friends, best lovers, or best groups to affiliate with.

In my case, one of my vampires (there have been a few in my life) was a towering, muscular, handsome young man who worked as a security guard at a bar a few blocks away from the one I was working at. As I said before, my life was all about work, so my hours were long and my social life was short. It was a lonely life, and I craved someone to come home to, when I wasn't working until the break of daylight. Furthermore, when I did have some time off, I wanted to enjoy the things I dealt in—good food, fancy drinks, and lively entertainment. These things were not cheap in Miami, as you may imagine or may know personally. If my friends did not have money to do what I wanted to do, I would simply say, "Don't worry about it! I got you."

This is also how it went when I started dating this guy—let's call him the Bouncer. He came with a sad story about life dealing him lemons when he wanted limes—having a son too young, drowning in debt due to child support, and having to work these kinds of jobs when he really wished he could have afforded to go to college. The Bouncer was affection-ate and full of compliments, yet sometimes aloof— which made me want him even more. He talked a big game about business ideas and aspirations. He also talked a big game about how much he liked me.

I was so hungry for that kind of attention and ad-miration. I was putty in his hands. We met up, after our shifts late at night, to go out or tried to arrange our days off together, here and there. We went to concerts, clubs, and even took his little boy to the movies. I thought we were pretty serious. The fact that he never had any money didn't really bother me. I thought, *He has big dreams! Someday it will even out.*

And his roommate! He had a buddy he lived with that was an obnoxious womanizer. I always wondered what in the world drew him to such a guy, not realizing at the time the truth behind my grandmother's maxim, *"Dime con quien andas, y te diré quién eres."* (Tell me who you hang with, and I will tell you who you are.)

So, I paid, and I paid, until I was even paying the bills for his roommate! I figured, *Hey, I have the money and am doing well, why not?* Why not?! How about because these two guys were bleeding me dry? How about because I wasn't paying anything toward my debts? How about because there was no real exchange coming from either of them? When I needed help, they were too busy, not around, and nowhere to be found.

It all became embarrassingly clear one night when we met up after our shifts had ended. The two of them, who also happened to work together, met up with me at my bar. His buddy suggested we go eat at the nearby diner. These were two bodybuilders, so they ate a ton—six-egg omelets, side of meats, toast, and, of course, alcoholic beverages because, "Hey! The sun hasn't come up on South Beach yet!"

When the bill came, the roommate shoved it over to me. I looked at him bewildered, expecting a contribution. He said, "What? I don't have any money."

My boyfriend just looked down at his drink, avoiding eye contact. I was hoping for some sort of backup from him, but I got nothing. I felt a rush of heat rise to my face. "What do you mean? How did you expect to go out, eat, and drink if you didn't have any money?"

He flashed a snide side-smile and said, "You should know how this goes by now. You pay for him and you pay for his friend too. Pay up, sugar mama!"

Maybe I had been blinded by the desperate hope for a serious relationship or the emotional comfort it gave me to have a few moments in my hectic week of what I pretended was love. I was devouring the scraps my supposed "boyfriend" threw my way. Maybe I just didn't want to see the truth. But it became very clear in that moment.

And yet, can you believe it still took me a few weeks and catching him with another girl to finally snap into reality? So deep were the vampire's fangs in me.

Anyone trying to do anything of widespread value, trying to change things for the better, trying to make people happier, anyone thriving in business, **and** anyone who is feeling like they are *not* thriving, not happy, not loved enough—all of these people are open targets.

Beware of vampires!

Throughout my twenties, feeling lost and alone, I managed to succumb to some very toxic relationships that nearly killed me spiritually, mentally, and physically—the subject of which is a topic for another book, another time. I will only say this: thankfully, the vampires I left behind, whose grips I literally escaped from, did not manage to kill me nor did they kill my spirit.

Others were not so lucky.

Be intensely wary of those who start with lifting you up only to control you or bleed you of your resources. You will know it when it happens because you start to doubt what is most important to you, your integrity, and what you know to be right and wrong. You may feel trapped, or you may feel guilty at the thought of leaving despite wallowing in misery, but most importantly, there is something deep within you that will tell you constantly, "Get out!"

Believe me, I survived and escaped my fair share of vampire dens. As a coach, I feel so blessed now to be able to help people break free from their own vampires—toxic, crippling relationships with people, groups, or even terrible bosses. It is never easy. Vampires can be highly manipulative and weave a spell of codependence that seems unbreakable. When this happens, here is my advice to you:

1.  If you're in doubt, circle back to your vision. Is this where you really saw yourself? Is this where you belong? Let your vision propel you forward.

2.  Lean on your resources. At this point, the L in VOLAR may be your only way out. Even if you have alienated most of your friends and family for so long that you fear they may never take your call again, I assure you that many of them will be elated to pick up where you left off and help you start fresh. I speak from experience.

3.  Refuse to settle. Remember who you are! You are meant for more. You deserve more than scraps thrown at your feet. You deserve all the fullness of love, success, and life. Do NOT settle for anything less!

If all that fails, call me—I will help!

## Lean On Your Resources Exercise

List out all your resources. Think about these categories:

- Education (formal)—schooling, trade schools, workshops, or classes
- Education (informal)—books you have read, on-the-job training, podcasts, speakers that have impacted you
- Physical Assets—money, stocks, bonds, real estate, etc.
- Contacts—familial, friends, colleagues, connections
- Skills you have honed along the way—dig deep. Think about things that you would not traditionally list, like conflict resolution (if you have been in any sort of hospitality or management role, you have learned something about this), sales, customer care, working quickly under pressure, and critical thinking.

Think outside the box. Think with the full picture. Perhaps you're a housewife with three children, managing a household budget, organizing schedules, and dealing with multiple behavioral styles. These are all resources you can lean on in the professional world.

# PART FOUR

# Actualize a Plan

**CHAPTER 18**

# Actualize a Plan

MAYBE YOU ARE A GREAT PLANNER. Oh, you can make a plan! Make it neat, make it pretty, even color-code it!

*But,* the pivotal question is, how well do you *execute*?

Perhaps you have heard this before: the success of a plan is based solely on your ability to effectively execute that plan.

So why do so many people fail in executing their plans? Why do you start a diet, a class, a project, or a business only to veer off a few weeks (or even a few days) later? It is not enough to take time to make a plan. You have to *actualize* the plan—see it all the way through, despite adversity. It begins with a good amount of research, then establishing doable steps with precise deadlines. Finally, the plan should be simple. The simpler the steps, the more likely they are to get done. They should make you stretch beyond your comfort zone. Like working out a muscle, stretching beyond your limits is how you get growth.

Here are some common mistakes when making a plan that could be making it near impossible for you to execute it.

## 1. You Violate the KISS Rule (Keep It Simple Stupid!)

Now, *simple* does not mean *easy*. I know we Americans love things quick and easy. It is no wonder to anyone in the world why we have one of the highest obesity rates, connected in no small part to the obscene amounts of fast food we ingest from the time we can wean off of baby formula. Nothing great comes from *easy*.

Simple means "not so complicated that you render the plan impossible to execute." You *know* when a plan is too complicated. You feel it in your gut, an upset in your internal balance. You look at your plan and it ties your brain into knots.

Get to know the difference between the uneasy

feeling in your gut that tells you something is going to be a challenge—one with risk, growth, and great reward in the end—and the uneasy feeling that comes from utter confusion, something just too convoluted to even wrap your brain around—an overwhelming sensation, like standing in the middle of a tornado. That, my friend, is a good indication that it is *too complicated*. You need to scale it back. Begin with a few simple, focused, and important steps.

## 2. You Make the Plan So Unrealistic or Unwieldy, You Easily Get Defeated and Give Up

This one is easy enough. You can be bold but also be realistic. This may take finding a balance between these two fine lines. Find that balance with research and data.

When I decided to move to California from New Jersey, with no money in savings and nowhere to crash for a while, I established a bold timeline—three months in that situation. I wanted the target to be scary enough to move me into action, but not so scary as to allow me to get complacent and dissuaded in the process. I got busy researching everything I needed to know about how to make it happen—I scoured rental sites, interviewed colleagues who lived and worked out there, and priced out the relocation down to the finest detail. You need time-specific targets scary enough, but realistic and healthy, to keep you on track. You can lose ten pounds in a week, but is that truly healthy?

## 3. You Make the Plan Too Obscure

Clarity and specificity are just as vital in this step as they are in the vision step. Keeping it simple means keeping it precise and concise. Lofty steps with no specific action, like "eat healthier," may run you up against a wall. What does that mean—"eat healthier"? What exactly do you need to cut out of your diet or eat more of? How much? How are you going to track this? If you can't track it, how will you know you are making good progress?

Here are a couple more I hear a lot while coaching sales managers and executives: "Make more sales" or "Get more clients"—what do these mean exactly? How *many* more sales exactly? How many clients? What is the number you are looking for? Just *more* isn't an answer. What does *more* look like?

I once had a coaching session with a client who wanted to get into the HR industry. I asked, "What exact type of role within HR are you looking for?" She looked baffled, had no clue. Well, that informed her next action step, for sure.

"Go find that out. Do your research and get more specific."

You cannot throw a target on the wall, expecting it to stick with no specific data to back it up. This is why analytics is such a lucrative career, if you have that kind of mind—I surely don't. But if I don't know the answer to an important question, I sure as heck turn over every rock, stock, and spreadsheet to find it out! Get specific about your action steps!

## 4. You Don't Actually Work the Plan That You Make

Once you have written out your plan, do you see it through all the way? A great plan with no execution may as well be a crappy plan. Execution is a lot easier if your plan is simple. By now, you should have a few focal points you can break down, depending on your timeline, into sub-steps that are simple as well.

When I decided to move to California, my vision was clear. I did all the assessment of opportunities and resources, then created a timeline for myself— three months. In three months' time, I had to figure out the money to move, how I was going to get work, and where I was going to live. That was simple enough right there.

1. Secure a job
2. Secure a place to live
3. Move!

Three simple, but by no means easy, steps. That was my plan. Of course, from there came the sub-steps—do the math, research rental options, convince my boss to allow me to transfer to one of our properties in Santa Monica, and get the money to relocate. The last sub-step was going to be the hardest one, and in truth, I did not have that one fully figured out until the last month of my timeline. However, I had a solid plan with simple steps and a target date.

Now I just had to work the plan.

## 5. Here Is the Kicker: Do You Give Up at the First Sign of a Roadblock?

Remember that song I sent to *Ugly Betty*? I hadn't heard anything back. It was almost Christmas and I had been hard at work, diligently actualizing my plan.

My deadline was to be out of Jersey by the end of February, putting me in LA by March 2010.

I figured out how much money I needed to make for gas, rent, and a few weeks' cushion. I was picking up shifts like crazy and selling everything I had of value—which wasn't much. All that and I still needed $3,000. I started to get discouraged.

Then my brother Michael posted a picture on our

fridge. It was the Santa Monica Pier as a backdrop to the sand and rolling waves of Santa Monica Beach, with the mountains behind in the distance.

"What's this?" I asked.

"It's your vision," he said. "This way when you start to give up, like you've been doing lately, you will have to confront your vision!"

"Listen! I've done my research, picked up extra shifts, crunched the numbers, and I still would need $3,000 to fall from the sky to make this happen!"

To which he replied, "Maybe your music will pay for it."

At which point I burst into laughter. "My music? My music has never paid for ANYTHING!"

I will admit, my friends, that I started to heavily doubt my vision. Maybe this was a crazy idea after all.

Then a few days before Christmas, as I was driving home from work, I got a call from an LA number. It was the people from *Ugly Betty*. They wanted to use my song on an episode! I was so excited I had to pull over! The lady on the phone asked if I had any questions and, talk about impostor syndrome, I almost felt embarrassed to ask, "How much does this pay?"

"Well," she said, "as the songwriter, you get $1,500."

I thought, *Well, DAMN! I have never made that much with my music! That sounds pretty good.*

Then she said, "Oh, wait . . ."

I started to feel deflated. Impostor syndrome

doesn't just keep you from reaching, it also looks for ways to validate what you keep telling yourself—that you're not worthy of this. Sabotaged again! I started to give into my negative self-talk that told me, *See! Told you it was too good to be true!*

She went on, "Are you the publisher as well?"

"Yes. Mitch Savoie Music Publishing."

She said, "Oh, well then you also get $1,500 as the publisher."

Folks, you got it! Three thousand dollars just fell from the sky!

Immediately following the news, I requested and got approved to transfer to a Santa Monica store within my restaurant company. I found a friend who agreed to help me make the cross-country drive with all my stuff. And you better believe that on February 28, 2010 . . . I woke up to the biggest blizzard to hit Jersey in years! Yet another *roadblock*!

My mother called me early that morning.

"I guess you won't be leaving today."

I said, "Oh, I *am* leaving today!"

Then I looked out the window—all white. My car was buried in snow. My brother had just woken up. He walked up next to me and looked out the window. We stood silently dumbfounded for a moment. Then he turned to me and said, "So . . . I'll get the shovel."

And with that, I headed out west!

To recap, here are **<u>the ABCs of actualizing a plan</u>**:

A. Remember the <u>KISS</u> Rule—Keep it Simple Stupid! (Though you may also think of this as Keep it Simple and Scheduled.)

B. Three Things in Three Months—List out three vital things you will do in the next three months to get you to your goal. Work from there.

C. Roadblocks = Circle Back to the Vision.

## CHAPTER 19

# Practice Perceiving

BEFORE YOU CAN actualize a plan, it seems like common sense that you must first understand the actual and potential roadblocks to the situation that's truly ahead of you and your goals. Having clarified your vision in the very first step, you should now know what your goal is in 3-D. You should have a great wealth of opportunities and resources from which to draw, should you need them.

On to the planning stage, right? Well, yes and no.

Before you figure out the simple and effective plan, you need to ensure you have all the real facts. Just as a computer cannot come up with a logical answer to a mathematical problem without full and complete data, you must be sure you are grounded in reality, with all angles seen and understood, prior to coming up with a viable action plan. This includes being as aware as you can be of all the roadblocks that *could* come up. Recalibrating is much easier when you are prepared.

The challenge with this is that sometimes we think we see the facts, and yet what we are "seeing" is only half or one-third of the true story.

Once, a friend of mine was trying to lose weight. She thought she was working on an effective plan and perceived that she was eating healthier than ever. Yet she wasn't losing any weight.

"I have been eating better than ever and my weight is worse than before!"

This roadblock often leads to a very frustrating and self-perpetuating prophecy: "It doesn't matter what I eat; nothing works." An erroneous conclusion like this could easily lead someone to give up on a plan altogether.

As a closer look, I asked her to log everything she was eating and how much exercise she was actually doing. The reality was that she was making regular trips to her favorite fast-food restaurants, frequently splurging on baked goods, spending long hours in front of the TV, and not actually doing much exercise. Additionally, what she thought were "healthy foods," like lean meats and vegetables, were doused in flour, butter, too much oil (even the healthy fats need to be measured), and tons of hidden sugars. See? The concluding perception—"it doesn't matter what I eat; nothing works"—from the misperceived data—"I have been eating healthier than ever"—was skewed because the data was skewed.

This is just one example of how we can believe a false perception. So how do we ensure we are actually perceiving what is there, and not a mirage? This takes practice. It also takes being honest with oneself. Consistent tracking is the best way to really see hard data, like in the case of implementing healthy eating and exercise habits, tracking your foods and movement. There are many apps for this and many types of wearable devices. But you have to *wear* the device and *do* the tracking.

The same goes for professional goals. If you track your daily sales calls, professional activities, number of hours spent on an endeavor, etc. and do it *consistently*—consistency being key—then you will start to see the real data. Some of us begin with a tracking system and then fall off. Has that ever happened to you? Did you notice that when the tracking falls off, so does the progress? Tracking results is key in business and in life to really perceive what is going on and understand the true reasons behind dips and rises. When you can truly see, hear, and understand the information in front of you, ignoring the "noise," then and only then can you make an effective plan to actualize and pivot when you need to.

So how can we practice perceiving?

## Learn to Just LISTEN

We learn more by listening than talking. Shut up and listen more often. Our surroundings are full of clues that we too often overlook because we are busy expounding instead of absorbing.

I once sat at a registration table as a volunteer for a professional organization. At that table, I watched my competitor approach one of my clients, chat it up, and divulge his whole plan for winning business away from me—without even noticing I was standing right there! He was so busy talking, and so oblivious to his immediate surroundings, he failed to notice I was *right there*, attentively listening to every word, though it looked like I was distracted checking people in. Luckily, I can walk and chew gum at the same time. Underestimating your competitors, or your current challenges, will be the death of a salesman.

## Learn to Be STILL

Take some time each day to sit in silence and focus on what is happening all around you. Whether with eyes closed or opened—just be still, focus on your breath, the position of your body, and sounds in your environment. With your eyes open, focus on the details around you—colors, lighting, trees, marks on the wall. This is actually part of an exercise I do with my public speaking clients.

## The More You Can *Perceive*, the More Control You Will *Receive*

When you can truly and easily absorb every aspect of your surroundings, including the people in it, then you will begin to feel like you "own the room." The space is **yours**. Anyone coming into it is in *your* home, and *you* are in control. This exercise is not only great for being able to command a room, but it is also applicable to being able to command your intake of truth. The more we practice truly seeing, hearing, and absorbing the facts around us—the clues, the words said, the things not said, the between-the-lines messages, even when we don't like what we are perceiving—the more power we accumulate. It may sound hokey at this point but bears repeating because I don't see enough people getting the point—knowledge really is power. Not just book knowledge, though that is important too, but facts and figures learned from real-life experience.

This is so important in business as in personal finances. I have clients who want to get out of debt. I ask them the killer questions:

- How much debt do you have, exactly?
- How much money do you have?

If you cannot tell me exactly how much money you have right now in your bank account and other assets, exactly how much money you bring in weekly, how much you are spending weekly, and how much debt you have altogether, how can you make a workable financial plan? Again, this is another example of true perception, via tracking and data analysis.

My husband and I were in debt over $40,000 at one point. Perhaps that sounds small in comparison to many Americans drowning in credit card payments and student loans. For me, however, I had carried debt like a faithful bad companion since I was eighteen years old. I never imagined there could be such a thing as a "debt-free" life. Yet we decided that our vision was just that—"Debt-Free in Three" (three years). We began by reading books and articles on methods of handling debt, like the snowball method— paying off one major debt with the majority of funds, while only paying minimums on the rest until that one debt is fully paid. Then, *Bang*! Take a win. Next, focus on the next biggest debt with your full attention while the others get the minimums.

I made a spreadsheet and got a budgeting app to track all the money going in and out. At first, this data collection process was eye-opening. We had no clue how much we were overspending on things like dining out and entertainment. We even began working with a financial adviser, though at the time we didn't really have any money to advise on. He graciously helped us anyway, with tips and recommendations, while also adding to the vision by talking to us about things we would do in the future through investments, like Roth IRAs. At the time, that all sounded impossible and far away, but we kept in close contact with him, even beginning a small savings plan in tandem with our debt pay-off plan. We understood the importance, as he so wisely suggested, of establishing a savings *habit*, even while paying off debts. He is still advising us today, though now he gets to play with the "fun stuff," like investing in the market and growing our Roth accounts.

Once we had all the hard facts, debt amounts, and payoffs, and tracked our numbers weekly, we could then make a smart and simple plan. The plan was to cut down on all the non-vitals—not cut out altogether, mind you. We still enjoyed vacations and dining out, but we did it in a much more measured way while consistently (there is that word again) throwing every extra bit we could at killing the debts. The vision, data, and plan were all clear. We now just had to patiently, and faithfully, *actualize* the plan. Every time we got an extra bonus or unexpected cash gift, I would get excited and put another dent in our debt machine!

> ### Mitch's Words of Wisdom:
>
> **Emotion is important—get the emotion of gratitude and excitement at moving one step closer to the vision every time you make a step in its direction.**

Eventually, with clarity of vision, facts, and an appropriate action plan, we paid off our last debt! And we did it in *two* years instead of three! During the third year, we had accumulated a whopping $40,000 in savings, completely turning our debt-to-income ratio upside down with both of us attaining credit scores of over eight hundred!

A funny thing will happen when your plan and actions are focused—the universe will align to that flow of energy and often accelerate your path to your vision. You just have to stay consistent, persistent, open, and aware.

Practice perception.

## Actualize a Plan Exercise

Think of your vision and formulate a simple plan. Start with:

<u>Three Things in Three Months</u>

List out three things you will do in the next three months to effectively get you to your vision or make significant progress toward it.

*Remember the KISS Rule, but keep in mind that simple does not mean easy.

Once you've done this, find an accountability partner. This should be someone you can check in with to discuss what you have done, what challenges you've come across, and what needs to change in order to keep progress moving toward your goals.

# PART FIVE

# Recalibrate
# When Necessary

**CHAPTER 20**

# Recalibrate When Necessary

SOMETIMES YOU HAVE TO shift mid-plan, and that's OK. Sometimes you have to throw the plan out altogether and start from scratch, and that's OK. Sometimes, even the vision itself suddenly changes. That's OK too.

Remember that time I found myself suddenly homeless in LA?

Well, I had gone to LA with a vision: a successful music career. I had made some in-roads, headlined some exciting LA venues, and even got featured in a local music magazine. By day, I was working at the restaurant as a head waiter, trainer, and sometimes supervisor—whatever the GM could throw at me because he knew he could trust me. He even paid me to rewrite the training manuals for service and bar staff.

At night, I was spending all my time and money performing, promoting, paying for backup musicians and rehearsal spaces—giving it everything I had and then some because I was not going to wonder "what if." Yet it began to dawn on me, although I would always love music and the stage, I did *not* love the music business—especially as a woman in a still very chauvinistic industry. Music wasn't just work for me. It was supposed to be fun. If it wasn't fun and I wasn't enjoying the process of putting forth my art, it was not worth doing as a career. I could do a lot of other things for money and do my music for its purest pleasure—on my terms. Just as that realization was setting in, I found myself suddenly homeless, with no money in the bank.

It was at that point that I found it necessary to **Recalibrate!**

My first step? As mentioned before, I went to my *thinking place*. That was the first step to figuring out how I was going to fly past this gigantic roadblock, how I was going to shift and flow with the changing tides. As I sat on the beach in Santa Monica, trying to steady my nerves and figure out my next move, a new **Vision** started to become clear:

- A fulfilling career where my talents would be appreciated and fully utilized
- Debt-free
- Money in the bank

The **Opportunity** was also becoming clear. My GM had often suggested that I apply for the company's manager-training program. It was a large, national restaurant group with plenty of growth opportunities and very generous salaries. Sitting there on the sand, with the Pacific roaring in my ears and the wind blowing away any lingering doubts, I finally decided to raise my hand and say, "*Si, por favor!*" I decided I would apply for the manager-training program.

More immediately, I had to figure out that little issue of finding a place to live! I had to find some money, quick. This was going to require **Leaning on my Resources.** It was going to mean stepping way out of my comfort zone—asking for financial help.

You have to understand, part of my childhood was growing up as a child on welfare, constantly hearing my mother chant how there was no money, the subject of money was very sensitive for me. Yet I was well aware I was going to have to get over my pride and my negative emotions around money if I was going to survive this.

So, I did. I asked a friend, Peili Chen, a native LA

Valley girl with a heart the size of a football field, for help. We hadn't even known each other that long and yet, without hesitation, she pulled together the cash to help me secure an apartment. She not only offered her financial support, but she also offered her faith. She said, "I am not worried about you paying me back. You are going to be the best manager!" Can you imagine anybody you know who would just hand you a substantial amount of cash, with no hesitation? I know some *family members* who won't do that. She believed in me that much.

Now you may say, *That's great, but what if I don't have such a kindhearted friend? What if that resource is not available to me?* Sometimes resources come out of nowhere and sometimes you need to brainstorm—list out what is available to you. Turn over every rock until you find what you need. Also, keep in mind what I have covered in various ways already.

### Mitch's Words of Wisdom:

If you often make yourself a great resource to others, you will find no shortage of resources when you need one. That is the farmer's law—you reap what you sow.

Thanks to this resource, and her immense kindness, I was then ready and able to **Actualize A Plan**.

The plan was simple (remember the KISS Rule):

## My Three Things in Three Months

1. Secure a studio apartment
2. Rock my manager training program, completing it in record time
3. Pay back my friend and begin chipping away at the rest of my debts

Within three months, I had secured my own apartment, paid her back ahead of schedule, and completed my manager-training program in record time!

Upon completion of my training, a crucial thing happened on my path to where I am now. I was assigned to the company's high-profile Beverly Hills location, which also happened to be one of the main manager-training stores. Since the GM I worked under had no interest in training or mentoring anyone, he quickly picked up on the fact that I seemed to have a knack for it and took full advantage. All the trainees sent to our store were being assigned to work with me and, while my fellow managers dreaded having to deal with them, I actually loved it. I discovered a passion for training and developing these soon-to-be leaders. It was incredibly fulfilling to witness my trainees graduate, move on, kick butt, and then call me to say. "Mama Mitch, I did exactly what you taught me—and it worked!"

It filled me with such pride when one of my trainees would quickly soar, getting promoted to GM of their own store, and being recognized as a great leader!

I started to understand a few things:

1. You can be a rock star in many different ways,
2. When you use your talents to teach others, you grow along with them, and
3. Helping people become happy and successful is the most rewarding feeling!

## Recalibrate When Necessary

Don't fear the changing tides. When shift happens, flow with it. My vision had shifted—saying "YES" to that opportunity led me into a career that would prove greatly rewarding, not just financially, but mentally and spiritually. I continued to grow in leadership roles across different industries—director at a five-star hotel in Beverly Hills, community association management, and regional director of business development in the construction industry. As I touched more lives in my various roles, my vision became more and more defined: to one day have my own business, to be an entrepreneur like my grandmother had been, to run a business that would focus on what energizes me the most—speaking, coaching, and training!

One of my greatest adversities forced me to recalibrate and ultimately led me to my greatest dream. I am living and expanding on that dream today.

Remember:

> **When adversity rears its ugly head,**
> **Don't ask "Why?"**
> **Ask "What?" instead.**

## CHAPTER 21

# What about Intuition?

**Some People Call It Gut, Some People Call It "That Little Voice inside Your Head"—Intuition!**

INTUITION IS YOUR INNER COMPASS. It steers you when you cannot see the bigger picture quite yet. It's what actually led me to L.A. It's the part of me which, when I have ignored it, has nervously watched as I flailed myself against a brick wall of self-imposed adversity and then whispered sadly, *"I told you so."*

   Think about the last time your gut told you something—a strong suggestion to do or not to do, and you opposed it. Now think about the outcome. Not good?

What is that voice? Where does it come from? That is a question the world's most renowned scientists, philosophers, theologists, and theosophists have been trying to answer since humans could draw on cave walls. It's a concept too many people have been arguing and even fighting wars over for far too long. I don't have *that* answer for you. I just try to be connected to my intuition as much as possible and heed its warnings and urgings. The hardest thing is discerning between what your inner voice is *really* telling you and what you *want* to hear.

When it gets down to it, don't you know truth when you see it? Many may pretend not to. These people are trying to see what they want, choosing to ignore what they need. But you know the true voice when you hear it, don't you? It nags at you, like a persistent mom. It tugs at your shirttails and skirt hems. It is the voice or the feeling that sends warning signals via tightening or spasms in your abdominal area. You felt it when you decided to do something you knew you weren't supposed to. You felt it when you first sensed that some relationship would end badly, but you decided to ignore the signs, only to deeply regret it later. You felt it when you turned away from an action or opportunity because it was too scary to confront, only to find that turning away made you more miserable than the fear you had before. Sometimes we can color the message with our own momentary desire—"No, really! My gut says chocolate cake is good for me *right now*!" Maybe it is. Maybe it isn't.

How do you know? How do you tell the difference between your intuition—the guiding light through the tunnel, past the roadblock—and your own, misguided, momentary craving for whatever it is in that moment that you are seeking?

The answer can be found through what some people call mindfulness, meditation, prayer, or just being quiet and clear with your thoughts. How to do it depends on your own process and beliefs and what speaks to you.

When I was studying acting at the Lee Strasberg Studio in New York, they had us begin our acting class with some deep relaxation exercises. They would have us sit in a chair, sprawled out as comfortably as we could get, or sometimes lie on our backs on the cold black stage floor. We would then close our eyes, relax our breathing and scan our bodies, exploring every muscle from our heads down to our toes, "willing" each muscle to relax. I was young and impatient, couldn't see the purpose of all this, and I was usually too tired from late-night jam sessions with musicians in my dorm to stay fully awake. Furthermore, I could not understand what this had to do with acting! I was missing the point altogether.

I get it now.

When I deliver public speaking workshops, relaxation exercises are what I begin with. In public speaking, these exercises allow you to get out of your head, get relaxed, and loosen up. In acting school, however, I now understand they were trying to get us to shut down our brains, relax our nerves, and tap into our actor's intuition so we could "act from the gut," and tap into real emotion. Tapping into your gut is a practice, much like yoga or playing an instrument. You can get disciplined with listening if you practice listening. The more you get accustomed to listening deeply, the more you will be able to discern between the internal distractions and the truth—shut the counter-productive voices and hear the real inner voice—*your* intuition. When you can do this, you will be present enough and calm enough to take action, even if it *is* a scary, risky, giant leap.

## Relaxation Tips

Here are some relaxation exercises I have learned along the way and use often to quiet my brain, stay present, and ward off the nerves.

## Body Scan

Generally, to begin, it is always best to sit in a comfortable position, in a quiet and undisturbed place. Close your eyes and willfully scan your body for any tense spots, beginning with your head and working your way down. I do this exercise right before performing, speaking, teaching a class, having a difficult conversation, or just when my mind feels cluttered and antsy. This exercise of body-scanning, feeling the energy in every little part of your body, even the inside of your teeth or your tongue on the roof of your mouth, can take quite some time, but is a great way to steer your focus while actively relaxing your whole body. Try it now for a bit. See how it feels.

## Thought-Swatting

Next, don't fight the thoughts. Many people fail at this type of exercise because they think they are supposed to fight the thoughts, ignore the thoughts, or actively block them out completely. The struggle implies stress in itself. No wonder I have heard people say, "I can't meditate because it stresses me out." Well, conflict would do that to you! Don't engage in a conflict with your own mind. Just allow for the thoughts to come, acknowledge them, and then gently swat them off—that's right—like flies! As those annoying little critters come around, simply swat 'em off, blow 'em off, send them on their way. You can even show gratitude and thank them—just say, "Okay, thank you." Acknowledge and then send them to the shredder. "You have been heard. Now go on your merry way."

It sounds silly, I know! But it works. If you practice enough "thought-swatting" eventually your thoughts will know better than to come around bugging you (pun totally intended!).

**Affirmations**

Another popular relaxation technique is to focus on a positive affirmation. Sit comfortably, relax, breathe naturally, and then focus on an affirmation that energizes you or that calms you. "I am well, I am loved, and I am at peace." Or "People recognize my value and will easily pay for it!" Or "I am blessed with abundance!" Whatever variation makes you feel energized, inspired, or calm, match your affirmations with what you *need* in the moment. I have my clients find the exact phrase for them by playing around with the wording out loud until it feels right.

There are many schools of thought and practices on meditation, relaxation techniques, and mindfulness in general. There is a multitude of apps you can download as well and you can easily research which app will work for you, try them out, and then—like any practice, workout method, or dietary routine—find the one that fits best for you. It may change as you go along. That's totally fine. Recalibrate when necessary!

## Thinking Place

Everyone needs one—a *thinking place*. This is the place you go to disconnect from the noise and reconnect with your inner voice. For some, it is a quiet cathedral, for others an isolated mountaintop or the dense woods. For me, it has always been the ocean. As a teenager, I would ride my bike to the beach, drop it on the sand, and plop myself down next to the ocean just to watch the waves, listen to the seagulls, and let my mind decompress. When I found myself homeless in LA, it was Santa Monica Beach that quieted my worries and allowed me to think things through clearly until the whole plan unfolded—VOLAR!

What is your *thinking place*? Perhaps you have a few. Perhaps you have one for different moods and needs. That's perfect! Your thinking place has to serve your purpose at the time you need it. If one does not jump out at you immediately, don't fret! Try some different places in nature, check out some spots near you. You will know when you have found it or when it has found you.

**Trust Your Intuition!**

Intuition will lead you to unexpected and marvelous places, if only you listen intently enough, and then bravely answer its call. Intuition holds truth and direction when we feel lost. You are never really lost. Sometimes we just encounter roadblocks and get knocked off the road temporarily. But then, when we calmly recalibrate, tune into our inner compass, and faithfully circumvent the roadblock, we end up somewhere we never imagined we would.

One day, when I was having a hard time at work at the hands of that horribly mentally abusive boss, I went to Zuma Beach in Malibu to get some perspective. As I sat still and let my eyes gaze upon the horizon, listening to the Pacific Ocean waves ebbing and crashing, a pod of dolphins appeared unusually close to the shore. They jumped and flipped playfully in the air! It was so beautiful and unexpected!

What a gift, an example of what life should feel like! Life should feel like those dolphins doing what they are meant to do—playing, jumping, swimming with their friends, and enjoying every minute. Not worrying about whether a huge predator would come and end them all in one bite. That was the furthest thing from their minds. Come what may later, right then they were living in the moment, *for* the moment. Why was I wasting time and energy in a place where I felt I wasn't appreciated, seen, and fully valued? Right there, I decided I would somehow manifest a better opportunity, one that made me as giddy as those dolphins at play! I also imagined that life would be so much more fulfilling if I could just find the perfect partner to celebrate with. So, I envisioned that as well, my perfect relationship, what life would feel and look like, doing what I loved, accompanied by someone to love and be loved by. It was a creative thinking process. At the end of it, I felt uplifted, hopeful, and clear about my vision.

About a month later, on September 12, 2012, after being prompted by intuition to buy some last-minute tickets with friends, I was dancing like a teenager at the Hollywood Bowl to the energetic performance of the Dave Matthews Band. I was so thoroughly enjoying the company, the wine, the music, and the rare day off from the restaurant! I was as I had decided to be—happy, energized, and excited! I soaked in the breathtaking views of the Hollywood Hills from inside the venue—life was fabulous! I felt a deep sense of gratitude for everything I had accomplished in less than a year, from homeless and broke to managing a Beverly Hills restaurant and making an executive salary! I felt gratitude for my good friends that were enjoying this beautiful day with me. At that moment, I was in a state of elation.

And then, a tap on the shoulder—a tall, blue-eyed, beautiful man towered over me.

"I like the way you dance" was all he could shyly blurt out at first before running off to his friends to claim the free beer they had promised him if he mustered up the courage to speak to me. He found his courage and came back after the show to talk to me and get my phone number.

Four years later, that tall, blue-eyed boy and I got married, overlooking the same Santa Monica Pier that had so magically and forcefully pulled me to the west.

Seven years later, I established *my* company— SavHill Consulting LLC—my own coaching, speaking, and corporate-training business! Immediately, I had my ideal clients signing up, validating my jump to entrepreneurship, and affording me the greatest gift a person could find in life—the gift of living my true purpose. There is nothing like knowing that every day, you make a difference by making your own way and contributing to the growth and prosperity of those around you. And I do it alongside my soul mate, with money in the bank and zero debt.

Remember the vision I had set out on at Santa Monica Beach—my thinking place at that time? My three important goals? Check, check, and check!

Clear your head. Stay present. Listen. And then, trust your intuition—it is your superpower!

**Recalibrate When Necessary Exercise**

Write down the answers to these questions:

1. What about my plan is working well, serving me, and helping my growth or advancement in some way?
   a. How can I maximize what is working currently?
   b. How can I take what is working to the next level? What would that entail?

2. What is **_not_** working? Why?
   a. Do I have a lack of knowledge on how to execute this part of the plan?
   b. Do I find this unnecessary for growth or advancement at this point in time?
   c. Does this truly align with my vision?

3. What needs to change?
   a. Once you figure out what needs to change, brainstorm some ideas about HOW you will do this.
   b. Circle back to the vision for inspiration or help with your focus. If something does not contribute to the vision, throw it out.

## CHAPTER 22

# Don't Drown In
# a Glass of Water

MY GRANDMOTHER LILIA often would remind me, *"Mee-chee! No te ahogues en un vaso de agua!"* (Don't drown in a glass of water!)

This basically means keep your perspective in check! Don't let yourself get overwhelmed and buy into the idea that you are drowning in a sea of problems, when really it's just a small, very confrontable glass of water. Or maybe it is an ocean you are facing, like the one I was sitting by when I found myself homeless. And yet, haven't we figured out how to cross oceans? The point is *you don't have to drown*.

This is a vital lesson because often we are not the masters of our own mindset. We look at a problem and see all the ways in which we are already bested before we even begin to fight.

Perhaps you know someone who lives like this. You can offer them a plethora of solutions and they will bat every one of them away with a reason why it is impossible. And that's the thing, people like this are constantly problematic, victims of their own choosing. Remember, beware of vampires. The "constant victim" or the "drama magnet" in your life can also be a form of vampire. I am not refuting that there are true victims in the world—a child being abused or neglected, a person giving in good faith only to find they have been bamboozled and left with nothing, a good spouse finding they have been cheated on. Have you ever been a true victim? Most of us have at some point. How we look at the situation and how we respond to it, however, is what makes us either momentary victims or victims for life. It is also what we choose to take away and **do** afterward that makes us winners in the end or constant losers.

Do you like to win?

We all do! Who enters a game choosing that they will inevitably be losers? Yet that is what some people are doing through life. They are constantly choosing to drown in a glass of water, living in a state of constant overwhelm, instead of looking at the problem and seeing it for what it is—just a problem. You know the saying, "Everything has a remedy except for death." There is always a remedy, or at least a way to live with the situation in a state of calmness, staying afloat peacefully until the appropriate opportunity comes along.

Some people have all the resources in the world and see nothing but deficit. If they can't change their perspective, they will always be wallowing in want, no matter how much money and resources they amass.

How do you look at your problems? Are they oceans or glasses of water?

When a negative situation arises, what do you tell yourself in the moment? All the steps in the VOLAR formula will not get you anywhere if your perspective is already set to lose.

I could have let myself drown in a moment of uncertainty, as I found myself homeless, changing clothes in a storage room, and figuring out from day to day whose couch I would crash on next, unable to see clearly what my next step was.

The Stoic philosophers believed that a situation is neither good nor bad, it just *is*. If you choose to look at adversity in this way, you will find a calmness that will help you stay sharp enough to come up with valuable ideas and productive solutions. If you choose to look at a roadblock as just that—something in the road to be removed—then you will find answers, opportunities, resources, and options. You will be able to formulate an effective plan and actualize it. And if that doesn't work, you don't throw your face into your hands in despair. You *recalibrate*.

Imagine where we would be now if Alexander Graham Bell had given up on the concept of the telephone after a multitude of failed experiments and attacks from nasty critics!

When I sat on Santa Monica Beach in a state of panic, I didn't bitch at the universe for being unfair. I had come with open hands, awaiting answers, decidedly hopeful that they were waiting for me. I sat quietly and listened for them. I had come in search of a new vision, clues as to opportunities I was perhaps overlooking, ideas of resources, and a plan to actualize. I was *not* going there to drown in a glass of water or an angry ocean. I was there to recalibrate and relearn how to fly—VOLAR.

And the answers did come. I recalibrated and took flight to soaring heights, thereafter. And I have helped many, many people to do the same since then, find advantage in their adversity, turn roadblocks into runways to their soaring heights. It is now my life's work, and it fills me like nothing I could have ever dreamed of before.

Sometimes you have to sludge through many failures before you find true success. That is why there are not a billion billionaires—most people give up right before the finish line, just as the big break is about to emerge! Or some stop dreaming after one dream has been crushed, mistakenly attaching themselves to the false belief that dreaming only leads to heartbreak or bankruptcy. How sad and unfortunate.

Remember:

> **When adversity rears its ugly head,**
> **Don't ask "Why?"**
> **Ask "What?" instead.**

Don't ask "Why? Why now? Why *me*? Why, God, why?!"

Instead, ask "What? What now? What next? What can I learn from this? What open door will this closed door lead to?"

Ask "What?" instead of "Why?"

Make the decision that you will not be the spoil of adversity, but that you will fly beyond it—VOLAR!

You can have the gift of living your purpose too if you are brave enough to fly. If you already have it, then you can help others attain it as well. Contribute.

Be the wind in someone else's sails and you will never find yourself lost at sea or grounded by road-blocks. Turn those roadblocks into runways!

The truth is if you can steel yourself, believe in yourself, calm yourself, and keep your eye on a true and clear vision, you *will* achieve what you have conceived! I believe this 100 percent! I believe in *you*! Go out there and soar to your horizon, and when you get there:

Stretch Your Horizons!

**CHAPTER 23**

# Taking Flight

I DID NOT PLAN IT THIS WAY. I promise I didn't. It was a delightful surprise when I realized it! When you set out to write a book—especially your first book—you just write, and write, and write some more. Some things don't make the cut in the end.

I didn't plan on how much I was going to write. I just knew I had something important to share and I wanted to make sure I was bringing value to people, giving a road map and the exact steps to follow to turn their roadblocks into runways to success. I wanted to take you on a journey and inspire you to dream big, find your wings, spread them wide, and *fly*!

At first, I didn't count the chapters or the words. I couldn't be bothered by those trivialities. I just wanted to say what I had to say. When I thought I was done, I realized I had just a little more left. One more chapter. I had to wrap it all up and bring it home to you. That's when I counted what I had and came to the exciting realization of where I was—chapter twenty-three!

Twenty-three!

Some of you sports fans may already have caught its importance and the beautiful coincidence—a chapter on taking flight—chapter twenty-three!

When I was a young woman, living in NYC in the '90s, I was obsessed with the man who made us all believe that humans could fly: the man who immortalized and retired basketball-jersey number twenty-three in Chicago, the greatest of all-time NBA basketball leaders, Michael Jordan. His story inspired me as a young woman, the concept of flying past adversity, and actually watching Michael *FLY* past his adversaries on the court! I respected the talent, the focus, the team leadership, and the way he always did what he set out to do, despite adversity.

But he did not do it alone, and I respect that even more today, as a leadership coach. One could argue that MJ's success was in no small part bolstered by great coaches, like his college coach, the legendary Dean Smith of UNC-Chapel Hill, and Phil Jackson, the Zen master of NBA coaches. Talent and big dreams often fall short without strong direction, motivation, and accountability. Number twenty-three knew the importance of minding his coaches, surrounding himself with people who inspired him, and as a result, taught generations to believe that we could indeed *fly*—VOLAR!

Chapter twenty-three is not just a summary, putting VOLAR all together for you. It is my tribute to all great coaches, leaders, and dreamers who have ever dared to fly or help others find, and strategically develop their own wings. I tip my hat to them and endeavor to one day be like them. It has been a magical journey for me so far, one that has led me to be where I am now—helping others learn how to lead with compassion, with strength, with intelligence, and with the end goal always in mind, all while growing the people they lead. If we all endeavored to help others around us grow, we would also grow by default. If we all grew exponentially in happiness, success, and great leadership acumen, the world would definitely be constantly improving as well.

Don't throw shade on someone's dream or ambition. Who are you to name that person's fate? At the same time, don't let others throw shade on your own dreams. You create your story!

I said it before—vision is what propels us forward

when adversity comes our way. Vision is what pushes us upward and beyond the roadblocks. But a vision without direction, guidance, support, and accountability often fails. Add to that, a vision with no element of contribution to others may not be enough to inspire you to act or help improve conditions around us. We all fail and succeed together. So, help others succeed. Do everything you can to succeed yourself. Disregard the nonbelievers and haters saying, "Why don't you grow up already?" or "Why don't you stop dreaming and get *real*?"

Yeah. Go ahead—stop dreaming and get *real*—real stumped and real miserable.

What if Michael Jordan would have stopped every time someone told him he couldn't accomplish what he dreamed of? What if anyone who has ever done anything to push our society forward had "gotten real" and stopped trying to make their dreams a reality—scientists, artists, architects, engineers, social revolutionaries, activists, geniuses, and everyday people who helped make the world a little better by going against the grain and daring to do something that improved conditions in spite of the haters? Every time you think your goal is impossible, lean on your resources—research, read about, call to mind someone who broke a barrier, someone who was the first to do something, someone who proved the nonbelievers wrong. History is full of them. These dreamers and their stories are part of your resources. *Our* stories are also resources for others who need inspiration and hope.

What is your dream? What will *your* story be? Who will be better because of it? How will you contribute more to society, to your family, to your own spirit and happiness if you dare to fly—dare VOLAR?

The steps are simple. I live by that KISS Rule (keep it simple, stupid!) But you have to *do* the steps and *do* the work. Only *you* can actually execute your own plan toward your dream. I can help you map out the flight path, gear up and strap in, but *you* have to take off. <u>*You* are the pilot of your own flight.</u>

How will you do it? Who will help you? Who will *you* help, later on, in order to pay it forward?

All you need is a strong desire and five simple steps—**VOLAR:**

**V**—Vision (Clarify your vision)

**O**—Opportunity (When it comes to your door, raise your hand and say, *"Si, por favor!"*)

**L**—Lean On Your Resources

**A**—Actualize A Plan

**R**—Recalibrate When Necessary

Visualize yourself flying. See yourself walking through newly opened doors. Feel all of the feelings that will come with your success. Get the feeling of taking flight. Believe **YOU** can fly!

See you in the stratosphere, my friend!

# Acknowledgments

It is impossible to thank everyone who contributed to VOLAR's journey. At first, I didn't want to include an acknowledgments page for fear I might miss someone and hurt their feelings. This book has been many years in the making so there is a long list of people who contributed to its creation. Know that I am grateful to you ALL! And I believe you know who you are. Thank YOU.

I am grateful for my friends, family, colleagues and clients who helped in many different ways along the process–whether it be through sparking ideas, contributing to the stories herein, or by way of offering emotional support.

Specifically, as pertains to the making of this book, I would like to give special thanks to:

- Those who were part of the stories and gave their permission to share what I learned from them.
- My husband, *Jason Hill*, for the initial editing of the book, as well as the continued support.

- My brother, *Michael Corrales*, and fabulous friend, *Fabienne Moore,* for initial eyes on the manuscript and invaluable feedback.
- My in-laws, *Sandra and Tommy Hill*, for putting up with me in their home during the final stages of this book's creation.
- *Angela Buttimer,* for her inspirational coaching and book development/publishing guidance.
- *Yaddyra Peralta*, MFA, published poet, editor, and Life-Long Best Friend, for countless couches to crash on along my life's journey from the time I was 17; for coaching me on how to write this book; for cheerleading along the way; for initial edits and ongoing consultation of the book; and for being my Soul-Sister For Life!

Also, highest praises and thanks to my editing and design team for taking my vision of VOLAR and *soaring* with it!

# About the Author

Mitch Savoie Hill is a first-generation American born of Cuban exiles. Having overcome a great deal of adversity in her life, such as childhood poverty, abusive relationships, work discrimination, and even homelessness, she now helps others leverage their strengths and turn their adversities into their advantage. Mitch is a certified professional coach, international TEDx speaker, and corporate trainer with over twenty-five years of hospitality and leadership experience. She started in the hospitality industry as a singing waitress in New York City when she was eighteen years old, and later went on to manage teams for international companies in the restaurant, hotel, property management, and construction industries.

As the CEO and founder of SavHill Consulting LLC, she delivers inclusive leadership coaching, corporate training, and keynote speeches that help her audiences learn how to truly engage their diverse clients and teams to achieve optimum productivity and success.

Working in high-stress, fast-paced environments and unique markets, such as Miami, New York, Atlanta, and Los Angeles, Mitch Savoie Hill developed best practices for dealing with different personalities and inspiring cooperation among diverse teams.

Mitch uses her charismatic personality and her contagious laugh to captivate her audiences and enlighten them on important topics such as conflict management, how to inspire cooperation, and embracing diversity, equity, and inclusion.

Mitch Savoie Hill is energized by helping people clarify their visions, map out actionable strategies, and stretch their horizons!

*"Mitch Savoie Hill is an absolute powerhouse. She is one of the most motivating, professional, energetic, and inspiring speakers I have ever worked with, and she has a*

*way of making every single person feel engaged and important . . ."*

— *B. B., Meeting Professionals International*

To find out more about Mitch, schedule a coaching consultation or book Mitch as a speaker or corporate trainer, go to:

www.savhillconsulting.com
http://www.linkedin.com/in/mitchsavoiehill